How I wish my dad had written such a book for me—full of stories from a previous generation, stories of family and place, childhood adventures, teen-age jobs and school, military service, church life, and earning a living! The details vary widely from today, but the values endure—love, duty, family, vocation, faith, hard work, sacrifice, fulfillment. I know and love Harold Brown as his pastor. You will find his story full of insights for living, circumstances that might overwhelm today, but forged character that beckons to modern readers. Along the way, you will smile, chuckle, and even laugh out loud at his stories. In the end, you will be glad you read his book and may even consider writing such a story for your children. I now plan to do so for mine!

—The Rev. Dr. James R. Fuller,
Senior Pastor, Calder Baptist Church, Beaumont, Texas

In *My Son: To Whom it May Concern*, Harold Brown provides a view of life as seen by an octogenarian looking in the rear-view mirror. It's a clear view, and compelling too, because an "ordinary" life well-lived resonates with other lives, probably even your own. Brown's son, Paul, isn't your child, but he may remind you of children you know. Brown's marriage to his remarkable wife, Winnie, isn't your marriage, but you'll relate to the life they lived together, accompanied by their family, friends and church. *My Son* is a Texas story of life and family and faith in the latter half of the 20th century. It'll take you back.

— Marv Knox, Editor, Baptist Standard

My Son
To Whom It May Concern

by
H. HAROLD BROWN

© 2018

Published in the United States by Nurturing Faith Inc., Macon GA,

www.nurturingfaith.net.

Library of Congress Cataloging-in-Publication Data is available.

ISBN 978-1-63528-041-8

All rights reserved. Printed in the United States of America.

Cover photo by Smileus.

Scriptures taken from the Holy Bible, New International Version®, NIV®. Copyright © 1973, 1978, 1984, 2011 by Biblica, Inc.™ Used by permission of Zondervan. All rights reserved worldwide. www.zondervan.com The "NIV" and "New International Version" are trademarks registered in the United States Patent and Trademark Office by Biblica, Inc.™

Dedicated to Winnie, to my mother, and to my son, Paul, whose companionships and love have blessed my life beyond the fondest dreams and expectations I could ever have imagined.

My son then

The intervening years!

My son now

TABLE OF CONTENTS

About the Author ix

Preface xi

Prologue xiii

1. Our Meeting and Marriage 3
2. Snow Time in Malakoff 4
3. The Ice Box 6
4. Gin Tank Baptizing 8
5. Introducing Daddy 9
6. A New Culture and Race 11
7. Hazards of Tree Climbing 14
8. Easter in Beeville 15
9. Joining the Air Force 17

    What's in a Name* 19

10. My Best Story 20
11. The Gulf Market 22
12. The Mail 25
13. A Baboon in East Texas 27
14. Ministry at Sabine Oaks 29
15. Seeking a Fortune in
    Scrap Iron 30
16. Beginning a Faith Journey 32
17. The Goose Hunting Lease 34
18. Baby It's Cold Outside 35
19. The Journey to Senior Buyer .. 37

    Money Trees* 40

20. The Senior Trip 41
21. The Wrong Runway 42
22. The Three 'Amigos' 44
23. Leaves, Leaves 47
24. Steak House Sign 48
25. The Centennial 49
26. Grandmamma's Week 50
27. My Earliest Memory 54
28. The Rose Parade 55
29. It Was George 57

    The Fourth Branch of
    Government* 60

30. The Fire Phone 61

31. The Horse Ride 62

32. Back to College...................... 63

33. Maggie and Me....................... 65
    Johnson, George W.; WHEN YOU AND I WERE YOUNG, MAGGIE; America Sings; Robbins Music Company, 799 Seventh Street, New York, N.Y.; Copyright 1935

34. The Hero 67

35. My Second Best Story............ 68

36. Brother-in-law Duncan........... 69

37. Hitch-hiking to Paris 70

38. Thoughts on Love.................. 72

39. Smokey Airplane 73

    The Songs of a Nation*.......... 76

40. Ollie and Golf 77

41. Pop and the Fresno 78

42. The Mexican Mission............. 79

43. Grocery Store Changes 81

44. A Little Lung Problem........... 83

45. High School Football............. 86

46. Another of My Stories 89

47. The Halloween Carnival 91

48. Churches 92

49. Christmas Time 97

    A Cause to Fear* 99

50. Adventures with Jim 100

51. Hitching a Ride with Don ... 102

52. Daddy's Demise................... 104

53. A Floundering Trip 106

54. Mrs. Blackwell..................... 108

55. Apples................................. 110

56. Rubber Guns 112

57. Pop's Barbeque.................... 113

58. The 3rd Grade 115

59. Being Political..................... 116

    "Slow Horses"* 119

60. The Ladies 120

Post Script...................... 128

*Columns written for publication in the home town newspaper, MALAKOFF NEWS, in 1960s.

ABOUT THE AUTHOR

H. Harold Brown grew up in Malakoff, Texas where the Baptist Church and school system provided a basis for his life. He graduated from high school in 1946, and was among the first students of Henderson County Junior College (Trinity Valley Community College). In 1948 he began a four year service with the U. S Air Force.

In 1952 Brown began a five year's tenure of Variety Store management. Marriage to Winnie Harris came in 1957. Shortly, he returned to an educational pursuit resulting in graduation in 1960 from the University of Corpus Christi (Texas A & M at Corpus Christi) with degree in Business Administration, minor in Religious Education.

1960 also saw the beginning of employment with Jefferson Chemical Co. (Texaco Chemical Co.), where Brown was employed for 28 years. The first 20 years with company lead to the position of Traffic Supervisor. The last eight years were spent as Senior Buyer for Texaco Chemical Co., Port Neches plant.

1961 found Brown beginning to use his Religious Education training at Southside, First Baptist Port Neches, Woodcrest in Port Arthur and eventually in 1993 to Calder; all Baptist congregations.

Other ministry services include: Shepard's Inn (a facility for visitors to area prisoners) and Triangle Aids Network (which primarily transported patients to Galveston and Houston for treatment). Calder church activities included Area hurricane repair, Mission trips, and Habitat for Humanity building.

Along the way he managed to work in 22 years on the Planning and Zoning Board for the City of Port Neches.

There is a tapestry of Americana in his life that, although not the same, is woven into the lives of all the parents, grand-parents or great grand-parents for the last 85 or more years.

PREFACE

I have written at various times over my years, but not published for remuneration. Recently, I read *Gilead*, a fictional autobiography of John Ames written by Marilynne Robinson. I began to think I might write about some of my own life experiences. I have named the writings *My Son: To Whom It May Concern*, and I suppose this to be a short résumé of my life, but much more it is the Americana of some 80 years in which I have lived.

I am 87 years of age, and the writings span time from the 1930s to the present. Those who have read my writings tell me I write somewhat like I verbalize the stories.

I have also included some of my stories and a few reprints from a newspaper column I had during the 1960s. They were carried only by my hometown newspaper, *The Malakoff News*.

What you will read are my life experiences, recalled from an old memory with the proviso that for some there is no one left to verify or contradict, except where I have noted otherwise.

H. Harold Brown

PROLOGUE

A Trend of Circumstance

When one pauses to reflect upon the many experiences of life, the unanswerable questions of "who, why, what, and how did all these contribute to my life?" inevitably enter one's mind.

"Fate," some would say. All of this was simply the destiny appointed to one's life. Such belief has long standing in the idea that the gods and goddesses determine the birth, life, and death of man. Seems to me that this relegates man to nothing.

"The self-made man," others might add. A person who has been especially successful in life will be pointed out and even held up as a role model. Most of the time this leaves out others' contributions. You surely could not apply this to me.

"God ordained it," some no doubt will say. There is no question that God, over time, has chosen certain individuals to perform life tasks of a godly nature and understanding. All our lives cannot be attributable to this, lest we be robots. And surely God did not create us to be robots.

Somewhere along the way, I have gravitated toward an understanding that most, if not all, of life is governed by the "trend of circumstances." The young child willingly jumps into the arms of the father, knowing that up until now this person has provided safety. Is it any wonder that as time goes by, the child continues to seek counsel from this "safe one"? As the "safe one" is augmented by teachers, friends, and acquaintances, we find ourselves surrounded by many "safe ones," and we are able to distinguish the "unsafe ones."

As a child learns to ride a tricycle, he or she experiments with speed and guidance, which is then groomed into confidence and knowledge that leads to the bicycle, the car, and for some a jet plane.

Circumstances consist of opportunity and recognition. Two persons may have the same opportunity in life. One will recognize and judge yes or no; the second may not ever see it as opportunity because the trends of his or her life have not afforded the knowledge to act in that circumstance. Trend of circumstance is like a never-ending, unnumbered series of doors. Life experiences up to any particular point, generally, will govern one's recognition of the circumstances (doors) as well as determine whether or not one enters a given door.

Trend of circumstance for me has a great deal to do with faith in God. Has one's acceptance of God as the "safe one" been sufficient to walk through some doors? At other doors, has past experience and knowledge been great enough to say no, close the door, and move on?

The trend of circumstance must also include hope. By this understanding the circumstances of life and challenges of faith must always be viewed in light of hope. By action or inaction hope extends beyond a particular circumstance. In the biblical rendition of "faith, hope, and love," an older translation uses the term *charity* in place of love. One of the meanings of charity is "the disposition to think favorably on others." Since the trend of circumstance not only relies on the remembrance of life experiences past, but also recognizes the life experience of now, we may say it also presupposes the life experience to come. These always concern others.

And so it is with a trend of circumstance—and hopefully the application of faith, hope, and charity—that I will bring to mind some small remembrances of circumstance. Some will no doubt be trivial in nature; others, perhaps, are of more importance. But all will lend contributions to the personal experiences that have become my trend of circumstance.

Join me!

H. Harold Brown

MY SON:
TO WHOM IT MAY CONCERN

1 Our Meeting and Marriage

I read a book recently in which a man wrote to his young first-grade son. He wanted to pass along to his son the happenings and persons that had contributed to his life. You are no longer a child, and I have grown quite old, but not unlike the fellow I just described, I have realized that I have not shared with you some of the things that molded and made me the person you know as your Father. I'll just write you a letter (it may be quite lengthy!).

I have shared with others how your mother, Winnie Irene Harris, and I came together and became your parents, but I do not remember if we ever shared the story with you.

Winnie and I both moved to West Columbia in 1955. She taught at the junior high school, and I managed a variety store. We developed a mutual friend, Harris, who taught at Winnie's school and attended the same church I was involved with. Harris seemed to deem it his duty to bring the two of us together, even to the point of aggravation.

Harris would go to school and tell Winnie about me, and then he would come by the store after school for coffee to tell me about the lady at school who I should become acquainted with. After a while, I knew who she was because she would occasionally come into the store. He was so insistent to both of us that he really made us wary of each other.

Finally, in September 1956 I came to the conclusion that I didn't want to continue to listen to Harris pester me about the lady at school. I decided I'd ask her to the movie. She would either turn me down, or we'd find ourselves uncomfortable with one another. Harris would be satisfied!

However, Winnie accepted my invitation, and much to our surprise we found ourselves quite attracted to one another. After our first date in September, Winnie and I began to see one another, and I gave her an engagement ring on December 25, 1956. We were married on March 15, 1957, in the home of Francis and Lucille Cates. As you know, our love lasted 51-plus years. Well, that's not true. Winnie left us at that time, but the love we shared is an everlasting part of me. Winnie was such a gracious lady as she shared all those years with me.

I cannot remember Harris's name, but I'm sure glad he irritated us about one another.

2 Snow Time in Malakoff

A few weeks back, prior to the time when I began to write, I was up at Little Elm, Texas, when snow with a little ice shut down my travel plans. When I was growing up in Malakoff, Texas, I do not remember having many times when it would snow, but there were times when we enjoyed "snow."

You see, "snow" time in Malakoff did not necessarily have the same meaning to some of us more fortunate kids as it does to kids around the world who look forward to the snowfall that allows them to sled, ski, and ice skate. The snow I refer to is artificial snow that was created when the scoring machine at the local ice house was in operation.

The ice house actually made 300-pound ice blocks from freshly drawn well water. The water was placed in large metal freezer buckets, which were then lowered into chilled brine water and connected to a hose to allow air to be bubbled through the water in the bucket. After about 36 hours the bucket would have ice formed all around it. The unfrozen water would be sucked out and replaced with fresh water. This was done so the ice that was formed would be very clear, almost like glass. The water was drawn out because it contained the impurities that were in the water. If it were allowed to continue and freeze, the ice would have white streaks.

After about 72 hours the buckets of water became blocks of ice and had to be taken from the brine bath. The buckets were hoisted up two at a time to be dunked in a vat of clear water. After a few minutes the buckets could be turned on their narrow sides, and the ice would slide out. The ice was then placed in a storage room where the temperature was below freezing. The ice was now frozen and ready to be prepared for sale to those requiring it for their ice boxes at home or for the soda fountain at the drug store. Some would be destined to be placed in the icing bins of railroad freight cars to keep the vegetables cool while traveling to Chicago, St. Louis, or other metropolitan areas of the country.

Not many people could use 300 pounds of ice at a time. For one thing nobody could have lifted it. The ice scoring machine solved this problem. The machine had three sets of spinning saw blades. The block of ice was first pushed into the machine while standing up ("standing up" means the block of ice stood about 4 feet tall and about 2 feet wide and 1 foot thick). As it was drawn into the machine, two sets of whirling blades scored the block at 1/3 and 2/3 of the height of the block. As the blades chewed into the ice, it snowed! All the chips of ice flew away from the block of ice and accumulated behind the machine.

The machine then turned the block of ice on its side as it was drawn along a set of blades that scored it at the midpoint for the length of the block. The blades did their job, and there was another snowfall! By choosing the appropriate score in the ice and using the ice pick, the "ice man" could provide various sizes of ice to the customer: 25 lbs., 50 lbs., 75 lbs., etc.

After high school I worked for a short time filling and pulling those ice buckets. However, I didn't last long with the 12-hour work days and only one day off every two weeks, followed by a change of shift to the other 12 hours. This was not very attractive employment for a growing boy.

Not everyone got to enjoy the summer snow. Those of us who lived nearby got to know the men who operated the ice plant very well, and when there was a lull in the activities at the plant, we were allowed to get some snow. On a hot 100- or 105-degree summer afternoon a big chunk of snow could really cool a person down. If you happened to gather enough, perhaps a small snowball fight would break out.

I guess one of the best things about snow time was that occasionally as you came away with a large chunk of snow, you could rush home, and all the family could enjoy a snow cone. You would put some snow in a glass, sprinkle a little sugar and a touch of vanilla (or some other flavoring), and top it off with fresh cow's milk. Very few people kept soft drinks or cola drinks in the home at this time, but I'm sure if there happened to be one in the ice box, it would be added to somebody's snow as a special summer treat.

Sometimes I wish all the kids of the world had just one of those snowballs or, maybe even better, a snow cone.

3 The Ice Box

Thinking about all this ice and snow brings back another memory about our old ice box. I'm fortunate enough because of Winnie's bargaining power to have two refrigerators and a freezer. We had just a plain old ice box when I was a kid.

Growing up within 50 yards of the local ice plant gives one an appreciation for the refrigerator that probably no one else had. The large engine that powered the ice plant used natural gas for fuel, and I believe it had only two cylinders, so when it was in operation, it had a distinctive sound. In close proximity to the red brick building stood the 30-foot tall exhaust pipe on the side nearest to our house. It was an exhaust pipe because it had very little, if any, muffler effect.

During the times of the year when ice was in demand, the engine ran all day, every day. We adjusted to the noise so that it did not bother us, especially at night when we slept with all the windows open to have maximum air circulation. Really, the big adjustment came during fall or early winter when the engine was run only intermittently. Quietness can be disturbing when you have learned to live with the steady and ever-present drone of an engine.

The production from the plant kept the community and countryside cool. The ice was delivered by the ice man, who had a weekly schedule for routes around the town and neighboring countryside, or could be picked up at the loading dock at the plant. The delivery man would load his truck with the 300-pound blocks of ice that had been scored so they could be broken into smaller pieces. After the truck was loaded, a heavy cover was placed over the ice to keep melting to a minimum.

The home or business delivery was done by the ice man and a little ingenuity. The home customer would have a small cardboard sign with 25, 50, 75, and 100 printed around the edges in large letters. How it was turned indicated how much ice was required. If the customer wanted 75 pounds, he would turn the sign so the 75 was on top. As the ice man drove along the road, he would see the 75, go to the back of his truck, and chip the 300-pound block with his ever-present ice pick until he had a piece that weighed approximately 75 pounds. He would clip his ice tongs to the piece of ice, back it up to the end of the truck, and carry it on his back. Each delivery man wore a leather guard on his back so he could carry the heavier pieces of ice without feeling the cold; it also protected him from the rough edges on the ice. For the smaller pieces he would just clip on and carry at his side.

The ice would be delivered to one of the most important pieces of furniture in the house: the ice box. Not all homes had a store-bought ice box. Some relied on an insulated and metal-lined box or perhaps a box partially sunk in the earth. The pride of the family that had one was an oak ice box with brass hinges and handles that had several compartments for storage of various types of foods and one top compartment that was for the ice.

One necessary aspect of these ice boxes was that there had to be a way to rid the box of the water as the ice melted. This was especially true for the ice box described above, which was too large to be emptied any other way. The furniture-type ice boxes had a drain for the water to run down a pipe to the outside, usually to the bottom. Many houses were built on piers, so a location in the kitchen, dining room, or porch determined where the ice box would sit so a hole could be made in the floor and a small funnel inserted for the water to drain into. This served well because the melting of the ice was slow enough that the water would be absorbed by the ground or evaporation would not allow a lot of accumulation.

Another method of disposal of the ice drippings was a drip pan. Many young men were rudely made aware of the necessity to empty the drip pan before retiring by being shocked into complete alertness early in the morning. The shock came as he hastened into the kitchen to start the fire in the cook stove. The 1/8 inch of cold water drained onto the linoleum floor came as a shock to a pair of unsuspecting bare feet.

It was an ice box, whatever kind, if it provided a place to keep the ice for cooling the perishable food, for the meal's iced tea, or for a summertime treat when we all gathered around and combined our efforts to freeze the homemade ice cream (but that's another story!).

4 Gin Tank Baptizing

In my daily early morning call to Carolyn today, an interesting discussion about baptism came up. I don't remember exactly how it started, but I began to tell her about part of my childhood.

You will remember that there was a Church of Christ located across the street from Grandmamma Brown's house in Malakoff. They had built there after two houses were torn down. Two or three of my boyhood friends had lived there prior to moving away.

What was known as the Church of Christ, sometimes known as "Campbellites," dates back to early Baptist history (1830–1832). A fellow named Alexander Campbell began a movement with Baptists of Tennessee. There were several areas of difference between Campbellites and mainstream Baptists: musical instruments in church, Communion, and baptism. The belief about baptism is what affects my story.

The Church of Christ in Malakoff practiced a belief that a person professing or presenting oneself to the church as a believer had to be baptized as soon as possible. They seemed to understand that until one was baptized, their salvation was incomplete. This meant the church across from Grandmamma's had to find a way to baptize since they did not have a baptistery.

Behind Grandmamma's house and across the road was an old cotton gin and a gin tank on Mr. Riddlesperger's property. The Church of Christ must have made a deal with Mr. Riddlesperger to use the gin tank for baptism.

As a teenager I frequently observed the consequence of the deal. If someone presented oneself on Sunday night or at night services during summer revivals, guess what happened? Early the next morning, the congregation would gather and proceed by Grandmamma Brown's house, down a lane, and across the road to the gin tank, where the baptism was performed. I believe they were lasting experiences, because occasionally some were performed in rather cold weather.

I wasn't baptized there. During the mid-30s the First Baptist Church, under the guidance of Brother J. L. Brantley, had a dollar-a-month campaign (that's another story) and added to the church Sunday school rooms and the church baptistery in which I was baptized (between 1938–1940—forgetful mind). I suppose the church records would show the date, but I have not pursued it. The fact that I was baptized is sufficient to know.

The First Baptist baptistery was much more impressive at that time because it not only provided a way for baptism in comfort, with warm water, but it also had a large painting behind the baptistery. Mr. Yates had been blessed with a talent for painting, and he provided a rendering of the Jordan River, where Jesus was baptized by John the Baptist. Thus, our baptistery seemingly flowed right out of the Jordan.

After all the baptisms that took place in the gin tank, Mr. Riddlesperger and all his brothers and their sons and daughters were Methodist and didn't have to be immersed.

5 Introducing Daddy

You didn't get to know my father, so maybe this will introduce you to him. Daddy had been pushed into adulthood at about 12 or 13 years of age when his father died. With a fifth- or sixth-grade education he assumed a great deal of responsibility and struggled to endure a domineering mother with six other children. He did it well, although I am sure each person contributed and shared in the family plight.

I came into the family at Quanah, Texas, during the latter part of the "Roaring 20s," joining a sister and brother. A third son followed a little over two years later. Dad's struggle with rearing a family led to some unfortunate decisions, contributing to some frustrating years during the 30s and 40s.

The first job I remember Daddy having was that of a lumberyard worker, loading and unloading trucks of lumber and ripping lumber to size. Very few persons had electric saws that could rip a 2x6 lengthwise or a sheet of plywood. This was done on a large table saw. Later, when he was introduced to the circular saw, Daddy had one kick back on him. He never, to my knowledge, used one again. There was little need during the 30s for a salesman's role at the lumberyard. If a person needed lumber or building material, he came to the lumberyard to purchase it. This was dictated by a rather dire need more than anything else.

Sometimes the lumberyard afforded services to the community that very few persons in the community knew about. One rather odd service I remember was when Daddy built a casket for a transient pauper who died while in the community. Of course it was just a wooden box, but it served a genuine need. I can remember that part of our family accompanied the deceased, along with a handful of other people, to a country cemetery for interment.

Another job Daddy performed one summer was replacing the seat padding in a Cross Roads school bus. Cross Roads was a small community a few miles south of Malakoff. There were four benches in the bus, and two parts of each bench had to be taken out for re-padding and re-covering. Each back and seat was removed from the bus and the cover and old padding stripped from it. The next thing to do was replace the padding, which was thick cotton. With the padding in place, an oil-cloth covering was then tacked securely to hold the padding in place. The back and seat of each bench was then reinstalled in the bus.

The late 30s and early 40s led Daddy into a related field of work when he became a builder/carpenter. He could replace a roof or build a house or an army camp. I know he could do these things because I joined him sometimes as teenager. I did not like replacing a flat roof, which involved the heating of asphalt, sometimes called tar. We usually did this in the early morning hours because as the heat of a summer day became hotter, it was almost impossible to stand the heat. This was also true of putting on asphalt shingles.

Daddy's help in building houses for war workers led me to share an experience with him as my first public job. A friend of Daddy's, Fred Johnson, was employed as the superintendent of a housing project for shipyard workers in Orange, Texas. The construction company was from Amarillo, Texas, where Johnson lived. Johnson had been raised in the Cayuga, a community south of Malakoff, and was acquainted with and related to a large number of people in the area. On his way to Orange, he recruited all the able-bodied carpenters for his project.

When summer came, my Daddy arranged for me to go with him to Orange to work on the housing project. I became the water boy for that big group of carpenters and construction people. It was really my first public job, although I had worked with him quite a bit and was paid for my work. Early in the morning, the large wooden barrels had to be filled with water and ice. In order for the men to have water where they were working, I had to fill canvas bags with the cold water and carry them to where the men were working and hang them in a shady place and provide some paper cups nearby. It was hot and humid, and all those men were thirsty!

For shelter we all lived in the completed or near-completed housing. At breakfast time and evening mealtime, everybody jumped on the company trucks and went to a small café for food and entertainment. I say "entertainment" because the song "San Antonio Rose" must have been number one on the country/western charts. The jukebox was never idle as the nickels and quarters were fed in to play the song. A café afforded us not only those two meals each day but also the sack lunches for the noon hour.

Here is where I learned one of my Daddy's most treasured characteristics: hard work. I think people held him in deep regard for that and believe enough of it rubbed off on me that I have benefited from trying to emulate him. He certainly sweated buckets full of perspiration in providing for his family.

6 A New Culture and Race

I have matured and live in a very different society and culture than that of my early childhood. This is especially true in regard to race relations. I am reminded of this daily as I read the newspaper and watch television.

The first African American I remember meeting was a woman named Evalina. She occasionally came to our house to help my mother do washing and ironing. Later, she was employed by a widow, Mrs. Fowler, who lived quite close to our house. Evalina and Grandmamma Brown became close friends and would occasionally visit one another in later years. Grandmamma had the greatest respect for Evalina as she raised her two daughters while living in the small house adjacent to the Fowler residence.

I also became acquainted with Mexican Americans in Malakoff, a coal-mining town that recruited Mexicans to work in the shaft mines. Malakoff Fuel Company, with the support of Texas Power and Light Company, built a community of housing in which mostly Mexican families lived. Other facilities were also provided: a Catholic Church, a store, and a dance hall. The Malakoff School District provided a teacher in the Mexican community to teach the children English so they could be able to attend the regular schools in Malakoff.

I remember interacting with some of the children at school. Two or three of the boys had learned to play the guitar and sing. It was a Friday afternoon when I first heard the song "La Cucaracha." Another remembrance is of a girl in my class named Florence Garza. I do believe she was the most intelligent person I have ever known, and I am sure she would have been the valedictorian if she and her family had not moved away.

I believe the town of Malakoff was exceptional in accepting the residents from Mexico and allowing them to find a place for their talents and physical abilities.

My closest connections to the African-American community came during my junior year of high school at the Gulf Market store. Among the black customers who traded there was a man named Washington; I think his first name may have been George. I liked to wait on him when he came to the store, usually on Saturday, to buy his groceries and animal feed in his mule-drawn wagon. I believe he worked for the Cotton Belt Railroad as part of Mr. Bradley's track maintenance crew. He always seemed to be smoking a cigar, which may have been his gift to himself for a good week. He was very casual when shopping for groceries and animal feed. After gathering everything, he would pull his wagon to the door where the feed was stored, and I would load the selected 100-pound sacks of chicken feed, cow feed, and/or horse feed onto the wagon. With a wave of his hand and a slap of the reins on the mules, he would be off toward home.

Jack Green, another black man who visited Gulf Market, was an automobile repairman at Royal Chevrolet and Buick located next to the store. Often he came during his break time to have a cold drink and/or a candy bar. I knew of Jack's father, Jesse Green, who had been the janitor/maintenance man at Alamo Ward Elementary School. I can still visualize Jesse sitting outside by the coal bin at the school. The teachers always knew where to send a child to locate Jesse when they needed help.

When the Air Force was integrated by order of President Truman in 1949, I was stationed at Keesler Field at Biloxi, Mississippi, in the radar training squadron. The idea of integration brought strong feelings within the barracks to which I was assigned. Many of the airmen in the barracks were from the South. There was quite a bit of talk that any black person coming in would be treated harshly; I even remember a threat to throw that person off the second-story balcony.

One afternoon a young black man arrived and was assigned an upper bunk in the second story. His name was Lawrence, and his bunk was two or three spaces down the aisle from mine. An unusual quietness pervaded the barracks as Lawrence began to unpack and arrange his gear and clothes.

As evening approached, several airmen gathered in the dayroom at the end of the barracks to talk and play cards. Sitting on my footlocker at the end of my bunk, I heard someone at the dayroom door call out that another person was needed to play hearts. No one responded, so Lawrence volunteered.

The young black airman passed me as he made his way to the dayroom, and I thought, "This may be your last walk." Yet something happened in that room that set the tone of acceptance for Lawrence as just another airman. The one exception was an airman from Indiana; I don't know why he harbored such feelings toward this young black man.

As time went by, various groups from the barracks played cards and went to the PX, movies, etc., on base with Lawrence. One airman from Virginia told me how uncomfortable he felt to be able to go to various places on the base with Lawrence but not be able to leave the base with him for movies, the beach, USO, etc. This was Biloxi, Mississippi, of 1949–1950.

Lawrence was a good student in training for radar, and I believe he was graded among the highest in his class. We learned he was from Chicago and that he had some college training.

After I came to Ellington Field in Houston, there was another black airman there whose name I cannot recall. He was assigned to the squadron orderly room and was in contact with all personnel of the squadron. He was from Pennsylvania, where he had been an outstanding athlete.

One holiday time (I believe it was Christmas) many airmen went on leave. Every airman had 30 days away from duty each year. Four men, including the black man from Pennsylvania, traveled by car to the East Coast for the holiday. On return one airman told me how ashamed and helpless the three felt as they traveled when the black airman could not use the bathroom or go into restaurants or cafés with them. He had to go to the back door or places marked for "colored." Many good things happened as a result of the integration of the military services.

7 Hazards of Tree Climbing

Most children, especially boys, find climbing a natural and normal part of their life experience. Since there was an abundance of trees in and around the area where I was raised, we took full advantage of them. I know one summer we spent a good 70 percent of our waking hours in trees close to our home. The following story is about one of those lazy summer afternoons and concerns only three of us young boys: Neil, my brother; Joe, our friend; and me. A fourth person played a part, but she never knew about it.

As I remember it, after lunch the three of us decided to climb up into a big oak tree about 40 yards from our house. This tree and its companion tree partially shaded the dirt street that led from the downtown area of Malakoff toward the rock building that housed the elementary school. The school streets led to various neighborhoods. The big oak trees offered a cool, shady respite from the summer heat.

The tree we selected was the easiest to climb because we could get to the lower limbs rather easily and, from there, move up and around on the other limbs to various heights. Each one of us had found a comfortable place to spin various childhood tales and dreams, summertime childhood pastimes. Joe and I had found comfortable places not very high in the tree. The bigger limbs down low lent themselves to being good for sitting astraddle. Brother Neil had become more venturesome and had climbed up into the highest part of the tree, high enough that the limbs were smaller and would bend down under the weight of his body.

It was Rita Mae, an attractive young lady who had recently moved into our town, who came strolling down the dirt road from town. All three of us recently had become aware that young girls could be attractive to us, although we did not choose to display those thoughts publicly. Thus, she was unaware that three pairs of eyes followed her every move. Under the tree she passed on up the street toward the school campus. Soon she had passed beyond hearing distance.

Brother Neil had made his way up into the higher reaches of our big oak tree. Rita Mae's passing had spurred him into action. He said, "If Rita Mae comes back down that street, here's how I am going to get out of this tree," as he began to climb along the outermost reaches of the limbs. As his weight caused the branches to bend, he began to slide from the higher limb onto the next lower limb.

We all knew the process Brother Neil used was the fastest way to dismount from a tree. You could somewhat gauge the speed of your descent as you passed from limb to limb. Then, finally nearing the ground, you could swing free and land on your feet.

At least that was the way it was supposed to work! About 30 feet up on the downslope of those limbs, Neil's feet became entangled with the limbs supporting him. His grip failed, and within a split second he was upside down and heading for the ground.

The earthen surface beneath that tree was bare, and in the summertime the heat and lack of rain caused the ground to become very hard, not unlike concrete. And that's where Neil's head and shoulders made contact after he had cleared that last bent-down limb.

I had never heard such a thud. Joe and I scrambled down. Neil was dazed. I thought he might have broken his neck, but the most evident thing was that he had the breath knocked out of him. My reaction was to pound him on the back to try to restore his breathing. I think he thought I was trying to do him more damage.

We got Neil home very quickly, and by some miracles of miracles he had no serious injury. It did not keep us from climbing trees, but I think it made us a little more careful as we played Tarzan or chased the bad men from tree to tree.

Eventually, we even got up enough nerve to talk to Rita Mae.

8 Easter in Beeville

I have written about how Winnie and I got together in West Columbia. Our courtship and resulting marriage happened over a rather short period of time. This meant we did not get to be around family and relatives since we were not in our hometowns. The next holiday after our marriage was Easter. Mom and Pop Harris were living in Victoria at this time, so Winnie and I decided to drive down for Easter Sunday.

At the time I was manager of the McLemore Variety Store in West Columbia. For weeks we would be promoting the sale of Easter merchandise: cloth for Easter dresses, swirly petticoats for the girls, rabbits (chocolate and stuffed), artificial grass, eggs (candy and plastic), baskets (filled and unfilled), etc. The Saturday before Easter would be a big sales day. This meant we could not leave West Columbia until the store was closed, the money counted and placed in the bank safety box. Then we drove to Victoria.

Easter morning arrived, and Mom, Pop, Kay, Winnie, and I traveled to Beeville to the home of Sidney and Gertrude Hirst, Mom's brother and sister-in-law. Upon arrival we found that their extended family had also gathered for the Easter celebration. Being the new son-in-law I was introduced to and, to some extent, informed about each new arrival.

I believe we had a normal family Easter. Everyone had brought their favorite dish to share in the Easter dinner. There was an Easter egg hunt for all the small children. By this time I could have taken a Sunday afternoon nap. Pop had other ideas.

Pop invited me to go with him to meet some of the relatives on the outskirts of Beeville. You know about this kind of trip because you later were invited to visit in the country. We would drive along, and every once in a while Pop would turn down a lane or into a driveway. There I would be introduced to, usually, a brother or sister of either Pop or Mom. Since this was Easter, it meant not only the couple who lived there, but their sons and daughters and grandchildren who had come for the Easter celebration.

I cannot remember whom all I got to meet that first Easter Sunday afternoon in the family. Pop, I guess, wanted to show off his new son-in-law or maybe put everyone on guard that there was a new person in the family.

By the time we returned to Sidney and Gertrude's home, I was about exhausted. We had to drive back to Victoria, and then Winnie and I completed the journey to West Columbia. By then I had developed a terrible headache and went directly to bed. Monday would be coming all too quickly. School would be awaiting Winnie, the store opened at 8:00, and all the Easter remnants had to be gathered and stored.

9 Joining the Air Force

In one of the earlier writings, I described an experience from my days in the U.S. Air Force. I have never shared too much about my Air Force time because so many others have given portions of their lives in the military service. A few whom I have known made the ultimate sacrifice of life in service to our nation. Thinking in these terms, my time and part seem insignificant. I will share a little of why and how I came to be in the Air Force.

As World War II came to its conclusion, the draft ended, and all the military services had to downsize. Most of the young men and women in service were anxious to get back home to their loved ones and have a family. By 1948 so many had left the service that there was talk of restarting the draft. Another reason may have been that there were a lot of young men who could not find employment. The military services could put people to work very cheaply.

My friend Jack Allen and I decided it might be a good idea to enlist and not be drafted. Work was difficult to find, and we realized that our age would put us on top of the draft list. By enlisting we could have the choice of selecting the branch of service in which we served. We made a big decision to go to Tyler and talk to the recruiting offices representing the various services. This we did, but even though we made no commitment, we did determine dates for enlistment. With this we returned home to think it over.

A short time went by, and I don't remember what trigger was pending for us to go, but as we talked, Jack backed out. When the day arrived, I packed a few essentials in a little travel bag; borrowed $20 from my brother, Robbie; walked down beside Highway 31 and hitched a ride to Tyler.

I was probably influenced in making the Air Force choice by a friend, Reagan Rogers. He had already joined the Air Force under one of their programs of training. He chose the field of airplane mechanics and maintenance. Reagan had already gone to Lackland Air Force Base in San Antonio for basic training. I chose to present myself to the Air Force recruiters in Tyler. After some testing and examinations, I was found to be eligible for enlistment and was duly sworn in as an airman.

Upon enlisting I was exposed to a new way of life, one that included being punched in private places and peered at in awkward positions. I remember there were at least five of us who experienced our enlistments together. After passing the examination and being sworn in, we were transferred to Longview, Texas, to begin the train ride to San Antonio and the Air Force training center located at Lackland Air Force Base, which would be our home for 13 weeks.

Arriving at San Antonio in the early morning while fuzzy-headed from a night where sleep was interrupted by clanking railroads and sudden braking, we were greeted by authoritarian figures the likes of whom we had never before encountered. The five of us were soon boarded on a bus bound for Lackland.

Shortly after arriving at Lackland we were, in a sense, herded and lined up at various places to be quickly "welcomed" to the Air Force. We had been joined by many other recruits who had arrived from all over the country and at least one foreigner, who I learned later was from Ireland (I believe his name was Rooney). I don't remember the exact schedule, but in the next few hours we received a series of vaccinations and shots, were issued Air Force clothing, and had most all of our hair removed. I had to go back a second time to meet the approval of an inspector station at the end of the line of barbers to see if my haircut was short enough in his perspective.

We finally arrived at the barracks, where the five of us were united with those who would share the experience of basic training as envisioned by the Air Force. We were also introduced to the two people who would rule our lives for the next 13 weeks. The main person in control of the flight (the term for the group assigned to a barracks) was a corporal. Within a few minutes he fairly well convinced us that his word—and the word of the other corporal—was law. This person's stature belied his status. He wore a blue and white military hardhat and stood about chin high to me. He looked up at me with huge eyeballs, and when he talked, you could see his two large upper teeth. He was somewhat comical looking, but since he mostly spoke in anger, no one dared to laugh.

I didn't have my picture taken very often when I was in the Air Force, but somewhere in the clutter of pictures around the house is a picture of a bald-headed, forlorn-looking airman sitting atop his footlocker: Airman Homer Harold Brown, AF18338471.

Harold Brown Writes*

COUNTERACTION

What's in a name?

Almost any endeavor, it seems, to be proper, must have some title or name. After some thought of the idea for a series of articles on the fundamental principles of government and politics the name COUNTERACTION came almost as a natural, as never before in the history of America has there been a time in which counteraction on the part of the citizenry has become so necessary.

To say that now is a time for counteraction is not to say that rebellion or overthrow is needful, but rather that a reversion to the principles of Republican government with Democratic representation must be of primary concern if freedom, as intended by our forefathers, is to endure.

In the second paragraph of the Declaration of Independence, we find: "Prudence, indeed, will dictate that governments long established, should not be changed for light and transient causes; and, accordingly, all experience hath shown, that mankind are more disposed to suffer, while evils are sufferable, than to right themselves by abolishing the forms to which they are accustomed." Now we must agree that our governmental and political atmosphere is not and has not been in the state of perfectness, but it has shown that it is sufferable.

We have suffered at times in economic upheavals; we have suffered at times because of sociological ignorance; we have suffered through periods of world conflict. But all this has been minimized when placed against the fact that the people, a person, an individual could still say he was an individual in pursuit of happiness.

It seems that of late there has been a growing attitude of a need for transition to a welfare state with federal intervention into state and civil affairs. Today we find that some would have us all pursue happiness at the same rate, at the same time, and in the same way. Now has come a need for counteraction.

10 My Best Story

I am going to tell you about a story I came up with some years ago. You will remember part of the real-life story, but an idea came to me from my early years of listening to the radio and television.

There was a time when the radio and television brought news, soap operas, and entertainment into our households. The entertainment programs featured such outstanding comedians as Jack Benny, Mary Livingston, George Burns, and Gracie Allen. One popular radio show was *Fibber McGee and Molly*. Much of their material was taken from real-life situations and then embellished by their imagination. So it is with what I consider "my best story."

Winnie and I traveled with a bus tour group that visited Williamsburg, Virginia. In making our way along the cobblestone street, Winnie's right foot was injured. It was a rather severe injury, but with the advice and help of the bus driver and various other persons, the foot was bandaged and the trip completed. Arriving back in Texas, a doctor examined the injured foot. The x-rays revealed a chipped bone on the side of her foot, so surgery was performed to pin the chip in place. This surgery occurred on the same day that a terrific hailstorm hit our area. It was bad enough to collapse the roof of the airport building. After the surgery a large cast was formed to enclose the foot and leg below Winnie's knee.

After a few days and with practice, Winnie was able to move around in normal way. We made a weekend trip to our place at Lake Sam Rayburn. Saturday morning, I broke out the rod and reel and proceeded to a favorite fishing spot. Our place at Rayburn was located on a hill and at the lake side was about 30 feet above the water level. I made my way down the steep incline and stepped out onto a rock projection that formed a ledge. The ledge had places where the water remained and a green, moss-like growth had sprung up. Stepping out onto the ledge, one of my feet found the slick moss. My feet must have gone up about head high, and in my attempt to break the fall, my left hand extended to the rock ledge, bearing all my weight. The wrist joint was crushed.

Crippled Winnie managed to drive me the 20-plus miles to the hospital in Jasper, Texas. After a quick x-ray in the emergency room, we were informed the hospital had no one with the expertise to apply proper, necessary treatment.

Crippled Winnie, again, had to drive from Jasper to Beaumont, a distance of some 75 miles, to the St. Elizabeth Hospital emergency room. God was good to us that day because a doctor was in the hospital whose specialty was in treating such an injury. The cast enclosed the hand and extended up past the elbow, thus requiring a sling.

You may now picture Winnie with a foot/leg cast being followed around by a fellow with his cast-enclosed arm in a neck sling. We tried to carry on our normal life duties, which often invoked comments and questions about our accidents: In the grocery store someone might ask, "What happened to your arm (or leg)?" at times followed by, "You need to talk to the lady (or man) in the next aisle. She (or he) has her (or his) leg (or arm) in a cast."

Some days later, the two of us were present at a meeting of the officers of our credit union. There was pleasant time for visiting and conversation as we enjoyed a dinner hour. A few questions or comments of inquiry or sympathy came our way.

As the meeting drew to an end, someone asked, "Is there anything else we need to discuss, or does anyone have a comment?"

I thought for a moment, got up out of my chair, and said, "I want to tell all of you what really happened to Winnie and me. Winnie will tell you that her injury occurred in Williamsburg, Virginia, and that I had an accident while fishing at Lake Rayburn, but this really is what happened."

It began early one Saturday morning as I went out to wash and clean out the car. Winnie had come into the front yard to work with flowers and trim some bushes. I finished my work on the car and immediately went into the house to take a shower. I was in the shower when I heard a commotion coming from the living room. I grabbed a towel, wrapped it around myself, and hurried down the hallway into the living room.

I found Winnie on the couch, and she was rather upset. The commotion I had heard was Winnie wildly shouting so all the world could hear, "Snake! Snake!" while jumping up and down on the couch. I quickly determined that she had brought a pot of flowers into the house and as she crossed the living room, a little green snake had been disturbed in the flower pot and had slithered across her arm. Needless to say, she had tossed that pot down and jumped onto the couch. It was clear that I had to find that snake!

Not knowing the direction in which the snake departed from the arm and tossed pot, I did my best. Finally, in desperation I got down on my elbows and knees to try and look under the couch. Then help arrived.

We had a little dog that had also heard the commotion in the front room and had come to lend assistance. That dog had begun to look under the towel that I had wrapped around myself. When that cold nose touched my rear end, I just fainted. That darn snake had surely bit me.

You can imagine that as I lay there motionless, Winnie wondered what was wrong. The thought came to her mind that I had had a heart attack. She got off the couch and made a quick sprint to the telephone for a call to 911.

Those people responded very quickly. They immediately began to work to resuscitate me. As I regained my senses and consciousness returned, they began to place me on the gurney.

Now I want you to really understand this, because this is really what happened to Winnie's foot and my arm. Those EMTs began to raise the gurney, and their understanding of what had happened became clearer to them. They began to snicker, and then they began to laugh. They let that gurney slip away from their grasp, and it fell. A corner of it fell on Winnie's foot. Of course, when it tipped over like that, I fell off, and in trying to catch myself, I broke my wrist.

That is the "real story" of how we got the casts.

At least I clarified this to the credit union group, and now you know the truth. One thing has continued. When I meet one of those credit union people to this day, they invariably ask, "Did you ever find that little green snake?"

11 The Gulf Market

"Gulf Market and Grocery" was what the sign said, and the big, round orange and black Gulf gasoline sign confirmed it. I was privileged to work there for a couple years during my high school years. I considered it the second best job in town. Weir's drugstore was probably the best job, but my friend Joe held that position. The difference was that the drugstore was downtown while we were located on Highway 31 and about four blocks up the street by the Chevrolet dealership. I think the drugstore paid a little more mainly because one could work more hours.

After school was out, Monday through Friday, I would toss what books were not bound for home in my locker and hurry down the highway to the Gulf market location, arriving around 4:00 PM and staying until the 8:00 closing time. Saturday, the store opened at 8:00 AM and stayed open until 8:00 PM. For this work I received the sum of eight dollars a week. This was pretty good pay for the 40s. I also worked some in summer when vacation time was due or the owner, Clyde Chapline, decided special cleaning was needed on the shelves or windows.

Small stores like this across the country served multiple purposes for the communities in which they were located. We had a selection of groceries, a meat market (we cut the meat and sliced the lunchmeat), a feed store (100-pound bags of chicken feed always seemed heavier than 100-pound bags of cow or horse feed), and we also had "Good Gulf" gasoline, kerosene, and motor oil.

One of my main jobs was bagging various items into small containers. Lima beans, pinto beans, navy beans, rice, and sugar came to us in 100-pound bags, which we had to sell in 2-, 5-, or 10-pound containers. Another item that was the most interesting for bagging was cookies. The cookies came in 25-pound boxes, which we then had to separate into cellophane bags that would hold about 1 pound each. These big boxes had their share of broken cookies. When I began working at the store, one of my favorite cookies was the Fig Newton. After having to sack a lot of these and taking care of the damaged and broken ones, I lost my taste for them.

I learned a lot from the three people with whom I worked and from those who came by to keep us informed of the community's happenings. Clyde was a World War I veteran and had been raised in New York state. He had a great kindliness for people and their plight. Several boys, like me, had worked for him, and he had urged us to earn college degrees.

Clyde was a bachelor, and he took good care of the elderly lady who kept his house. Whether he roomed there or owned the house I never knew. The lady had two prominent sons in the community, but Clyde seemed to take care of the lady and her requirements.

As I worked there, I became aware of Clyde's help to various persons who had experienced financial difficulty. We ran charge accounts at the store for a rather large number of persons. I know Clyde had a little journal in which he entered a person's debt that had become overdue and they did not come around anymore. Some people had simply had bad circumstances and were unable to pay, and others had tried to live above their means. I was aware of one person who had been rather respected in the community whose his children had gone to some of the finest colleges, but he had gone from town with a large debt owed to Clyde's store. He was one who did come back occasionally and make payment. I understand he finally paid off the entire bill. Even though some of these people had taken advantage of Clyde, I never heard him direct a bad comment toward any of these.

Claude was another Gulf employee. Also a veteran of World War I, he had been wounded, maybe even slightly gassed (the Germans used chlorine, I believe). I guess I remember Claude best because of his music ability. I don't mean he was an accomplished musician, but he was an example of how mankind will seek ways to use their talents. Claude learned music, as did many others of his generation, in music schools. This means he sang by what is known as shaped notes. His wife played piano in the same manner and played for the First Baptist Church for some time. Claude would take a new song (he sang bass), run through do-re-mi a few times, and he was ready to sing the song. To make the family complete musically, Claude's daughter, Laveral, was much in demand as soloist at church and school functions. I am sure she had been schooled in round-note music at school but probably got her start with the shaped notes. Claude was the one in charge when Clyde had to be away.

And then there was Fred Covert ("the old Irishman"). Maybe it is more proper to say "Mr. Fred" because he was older, a veteran of the Spanish-American War. Even as old as he was, probably late 60s or early 70s, he could still load a sack of feed on a wagon or a truck. Fred had two fingers missing on his right hand; I think they were shot off during the war, but whether he did it or the enemy did it, I am not sure. Even with those fingers missing, his handwriting was flawless. He served in the Philippine Islands and had been the company clerk. This meant he had to write the entire roster of the company each day of the week to show they were present for duty.

After his Army discharge Fred had worked for Bewley Mills, a flour company, as a clerk. The Bewley Mills 25- and 50-pound bags of flour had a signature of the man who had started the mills. I believe his name was J. W. Bewley. Mr. Fred could write that signature better than the one on the flour sacks.

One of the prides that Fred talked about occasionally was a son who was in the Air Force in England. He told about how the son had helped the Air Force return the bombers to service after the raids over Germany. The son had come up with an idea whereby the spark plugs could be cooled, in the hot engine, removed and replaced. Before his idea the engine had to be allowed to cool down, which required some length of time during which the plane would be out of service.

I learned a lot from these three men. Adding to their experience were those other men who came by during summer to have a cold drink or during winter to sit around the wood stove at the front of the store. All the community gossip and news were shared and even occasionally a big political situation, maybe not solved, but really discussed and cussed.

After work sometimes, my friend Lewis, who had a car, would come by. We would put in five gallons of that Good Gulf gasoline for 19 cents per gallon, and then we would go pick up our high school sweethearts. To call up that girl for the date, I would have to use the one phone in the store; it was located on the wall next to the meeting place where the cold drinks were consumed and the stove was located. My love life was open to all who cared to listen.

12 The Mail

Communication has always been important in the advancement of civilization. A letter carried forth by a 3-cent stamp was important during the 1940s. In a community like my hometown of Malakoff, Texas, there was no door-to-door delivery. The only exception was for those who happened to live on a rural route. They received their mail by delivery to the mailbox that had been mounted on a wooden post by the side of their country road.

The mail arrived in Malakoff twice daily by the Cotton Belt passenger train—one westbound and one eastbound. Bob Johnson, the community's shoe repairman, was also employed to meet each train for mail exchange.

Johnson would report to the back door of the post office 10 or 15 minutes prior to the trains' scheduled arrival. He would get his two-wheeled cart up close to the door, and the mail clerks inside the post office would toss out to him the locked gray bags containing all the outbound mail, including letters, papers, and small packages. The two-wheeled cart was for transporting the mail bags from the post office to the train depot about two blocks from the post office. The cart had rather large wheels, and the bed was mounted on the axle with two legs out toward the push handle. The bed was approximately 4 feet x 4 feet with a retaining board around the circumference. Many mail bags could be transported quite easily.

Arriving at the depot, Johnson would station the cart at a particular spot along the railroad tracks, depending on the direction of the arriving train. The mail car of the train would usually be stopped quite close to the mail cart. As the train slowed to a stop, Johnson pushed the cart so it would be located adjacent to the large door of the mail car. A bit of friendly chatter ensued as the outbound mail bags were tossed into the open door. Just as quickly from within the mail car, attendants would throw out the mail bags containing Malakoff's and the rural route's mail and small packages to the waiting Bob Johnson.

Once all the bags had been passed between cart and train car and those inbound secured on the two-wheel cart, Johnson hurried back to the post office. He would knock on the door, would be flung open so the mail bags could be passed quickly to the waiting mail clerks. Johnson then secured the mail cart and returned to his shoe repair business.

Certain things happened inside the post office when Johnson arrived. All the frosted glass windows—general delivery, saving stamps, and stamp sales—would be closed. The clerks and postmaster busied themselves in the internal distribution of the letters and packages. The rental boxes received designated letters and/or package notices. All letters and packages designated for general delivery were processed to an alphabetically divided file.

The mail arrival was quite a community event, especially during World War II. Each mail arrival stirred the hopes and fears in the hearts of wives, mothers, and sweethearts for a letter from their serviceman or war worker. The most nervous, perhaps, were the young men who had recently had their draft status changed. If they had been classified 1A, it meant a notice of a call to active duty would arrive soon.

If the gathered crowd became too noisy, the door with a frosted panel would be flung open, and the postmaster, Mr. Truelove, would yell out for all to hear, "If you people don't quiet down out here, the windows will not be opened!" The door would close, and all the noise would cease.

When all the mail had been processed and was ready for delivery, the frosted windows would be reopened. To those with a rental box, it was a sign that all the mail had been put up and they could check their box. Many of the boxes had small glass inserts so one could determine if mail had been delivered.

Those not having a rental box had to line up at the "general delivery" window. As each person became first in line, either the clerk knew his name or a name had to be given to the clerk. The clerk would retrieve the alphabetical file containing the person's last name and each letter in the file reviewed to see if there were letters or packages for that person.

The mail did not come door to door, but I think the community knew our neighbors and townspeople a little bit better. What more could you expect for a 3-cent stamp?

13 A Baboon in East Texas

You have been around me all of your life and have no doubt observed that I am not a very humorous. I enjoy a good story, either to tell or to hear, but I just don't laugh a lot. Following is one I heard and enjoyed.

The story was told by a judge from an East Texas county seat. I cannot recall the county or the judge's name, but he had gained a reputation as an after-dinner speaker. This story was enjoyed by a large group of people back in the 60s and 70s, but I am afraid the younger generation would have difficulty picturing the situation. I believe you will be able to understand.

A traveling carnival had come to one of the county seats in East Texas. It had all the attractions of many traveling carnivals: Ferris wheel, air rifle shooting gallery, baseball toss at the milk bottles, etc. The arrival of these traveling carnivals was special back in those days. I remember them coming to Athens, especially around the Old Fiddlers Contest that was held each year in May or June.

This particular carnival had an unusual attraction: a baboon. People in East Texas just didn't get to see a baboon very often. I suppose the people may have read or heard about such an animal, but to see one was an experience. The crowds came not only from the county seat town but from the surrounding communities as well. I believe teachers may have brought their classes to view this wild animal from a foreign country.

After the engagement in the county seat was complete, the carnival people began to pack up and move on the next county seat. Shortly after beginning the trip, the carnival people realized the baboon was ill. Their attempts to meet the needs for a cure were hopeless; the baboon died. I'm sure they questioned the cause of death: children had fed it something or the activity surrounding it was just too much, etc. Whatever the cause, their baboon was dead, and they had a dead body to deal with.

Now, when you have a dead baboon on your hands in East Texas, this becomes a formidable problem. What do you do with the body? You just cannot have a wagon weighted down with a dead baboon. It so happened that as they drove along, the road ran through a heavily forested area. The decision was made to unload the baboon and drag it off into the woods some distance away from the road.

Early next morning, the county EPA (a self-appointed group that took care of recently deceased birds and animals of the area) was in aggregate circling where the baboon's body had been placed. Roadkill on a road mostly traveled by wagons was few and far between, so this was a great attraction for those who normally took care of such situations. This activity drew the attention of two woodcutters traveling along the road, and they decided to investigate.

When the woodcutters arrived under the trees encircled by the EPA, they saw this "thing" lying there "dead as a mackerel," to use an East Texas term. As they looked, they determined it was nothing they had seen before. After a discussion they determined to load the "thing" on their wagon and carry it to have it identified.

Pulling their wagon up to the small local store and gas station, the woodcutters inquired of those nearby as to what they had on the wagon. No one knew.

After much discussion by those gathered around the wagon, a decision was made to seek the expertise of Uncle Jim Tanner, who sat on the front porch of the store as he had for years. Uncle Jim was nearly 100 years old and had seen or heard just about everything.

Uncle Jim came down to the wagon, and he walked around and viewed the body from every angle. After due consideration he shoved his straw hat back on his head, took his crook-stemmed pipe in his hand, wiped his brow with his red-checkered handkerchief, and "allowed" (that's when one comes forth with a learned observation), "I believe what you got here, after seeing that deep-furrowed brow and that reddened rear end, is one of those checker players that sit on the bandstand over at the county courthouse square." Everyone shook their head in agreement.

Best as I remember the story, no one in that group gathered around the woodcutters' wagon ever questioned Uncle Jim's conclusion.

Today's generation could not enjoy this story because they do not know about courthouse squares, wagons, and country stores. I believe you have a slight remembrance.

14 Ministry at Sabine Oaks

As you know, in my later years, beginning in 1999 and continuing for 15 years, I went each Sunday morning to an assisted-living facility called Sabine Oaks in Beaumont, Texas, where I would do a short worship service for the residents.

Your mother and I had begun attending Calder Baptist Church in Beaumont, and one of the ministries I became part of was doing this type of worship service. It worked rather handily, as I would drive Winnie to Calder, where she taught a Sunday school class, and I would go to Sabine Oaks to do about 45 minutes of worship time and then return to Calder for the worship service there.

I don't remember if it was the first day I went to Sabine Oaks, but early on Mrs. Jones became a regular at worship time. Every Sunday when I arrived, Mrs. Jones would be sitting in her wheelchair in the hallway just outside the worship center. This was true for many years.

Mrs. Jones was known as "the turtle lady" by everyone around Sabine Oaks because her room was decorated and displayed with many collectible turtles (not live). Kay, Winnie's sister, visited with me one Sunday and became inspired to return to Corpus and make me a quilted turtle pillow.

Some years passed before I received a phone call one day from the administrator at Sabine Oaks. Mrs. Jones had expired, and her daughter wanted "Father Brown" to be part of the funeral service. I agreed and took part in the service as requested and received a very nice note from the daughter later on.

"Father Brown"—now that's a name I never expected to hear! When I began the worship at Sabine Oaks, I determined that I would not reveal my denomination or church affiliation unless someone asked. I became aware that the small group that worshiped at Sabine Oaks was from many different faith groups. It worked well with Mrs. Jones, who accepted me as a representative of her Catholic faith as we worshiped all those years.

15 Seeking a Fortune in Scrap Iron

War is dreadful and wasteful. It removes so many from a community like my hometown. Some go away to help in the construction of wartime facilities; others serve in the armed forces. Those who remain at home are ever mindful to support and provide some of the needs of those who have gone away.

Women's organizations formed special groups to gather and make items such as bandages. Community leaders promoted and sponsored gatherings for the sale of war stamps and bonds that provided the federal government with money to fund the war effort. Collections of various items were made for their reuse, such as tin foil, tin cans, and paper. One of the most needful collections was that of scrap iron. It was valuable enough that money was paid at a central collection place to those willing to gather it.

This is where my story starts: Two energetic and financially strapped youngsters set out to try to supplement the small monies their respective parents were able to provide. They had made a few cents from collecting and returning soft drink bottles and earned some by mowing yards. We didn't have too many lawns in those days. How better to gain financial success than collecting and selling scrap iron? This was the way to untold wealth.

After a little thought and mind searching, Joe and I soon arrived at the conclusion that the Cotton Belt Railroad tracks would provide a productive place to begin our scrap-iron collection venture. We had been around the depot and tracks that cut through the heart of our town. We knew there were numerous bent rail spikes, damaged rail bolts and nuts, and occasionally discarded tie plates along the railroad right-of-way. These, as far as we knew, had accumulated along the tracks for years.

How do you collect this scrap-iron wealth? You get a couple five-gallon, handled buckets and set out down the tracks. Here a bolt, there a bolt, a spike, and before long you know you have struck the motherlode of scrap iron. It did not take long before the buckets began to weigh on the collectors. I mean really weigh. About three-quarters of a mile out of town, it became rather clear the motherlode was paying off. By the time we reached the Rogers property east of town, we concluded that we had reached our load limit.

It was quite a struggle to get those buckets of bolts and nuts the quarter mile from the railroad tracks, through the Rogers' field and orchard, to their house. Jean and Mrs. Rogers were quite cordial and treated us to a cool drink of water. I am sure they were skeptical of these two heat-stroked kids with two buckets of bolts.

The Rogers' property fronted on Highway 31, the main highway running between Malakoff and Athens, which was to be our travel route back to town. Thank goodness we were fortunate that someone came along and offered us a ride, along with our accumulated fortune, back to Malakoff. We made our first scrap-iron sale! Imagine our surprise when we each received about 15 cents apiece. We immediately made our way down to the local drugstore and treated ourselves to a Coke and a bag of Tom's peanuts.

Our next step was to consider some other enterprise to pursue for our fame and fortune. One of the major decisions was to determine the appropriate direction to travel if the enterprise concerned a weighty product.

16 Beginning a Faith Journey

I have written about my baptism, but we know that is the way the Baptist faith group allows a person to portray his or her belief in a risen Christ. The belief or faith journey is begun sometime prior to that activity.

I was raised attending the First Baptist Church of Malakoff, Texas. My first remembrances were of a white church building and a bell tower on the right front entrance to the church. Inside was a high ceiling with several fans that dropped down 10 or 12 feet below the ceiling. Each side had windows 8 or 10 feet in height that could be opened in summer for a cross-draft. This was before the church was blessed with air conditioning, which did come later.

In the 30s the church was led to remodel the building and add a two-story addition to the rear of the building. The addition offered a place for Sunday school rooms and a large area for dinners or class parties. As I remember, Daddy wasn't too enthusiastic about this room, as he did not think it proper to have much eating at church. I don't know why, because I believe he enjoyed what was called having "dinner on the ground." The church now was enclosed by brick of a soft yellow tint. This was the building where the previously mentioned baptism took place.

A practice of most Baptist churches, as well as our Methodist brethren, was that of having revivals annually and sometimes twice a year. This was an evangelistic-driven time for the church and usually involved inviting persons from outside the local church to lead. Usually this would be a song leader and an evangelist, and they would come for two weeks of services. There would be morning and evening services Sunday through Friday each week. As noted, these were evangelical meetings where, mostly, church members were reminded of sin and hell, with a special emphasis on smoking and drinking.

Most of the non-church members attending were like me. They came to Sunday school and other age-appropriate functions at church were encouraged to attend these revival services. The pastor and Sunday school teachers hoped and, I believe, prayed that children and non-church members would make a profession of faith (be born again, believe, be saved, etc.).

I don't remember the exact date I could point to for having such an experience, but when I was about 11 or 12, I had listened to enough sermons, Sunday school lessons, and other teachings that I did believe in and on Jesus as the Christ. The next step—and the most frightening thing for me—was presenting myself to the church.

Of course, this was in the middle of a summer morning revival service, and I had wrestled with my decision for a couple days; that aisle leading to the front was so awfully long. During the revival we boys usually sat near the back of the auditorium. I finally made it to the front to present myself to Brother Brantley (that is the way everyone spoke of their pastors back in those days). Brother Wilkes was the evangelist as I remember. He and the pastor had been an evangelist team prior to Brother Brantley coming as our pastor.

Neil followed me down the aisle. This is one thing I have long questioned in my mind all these years. Brother Brantley, somewhere in his comments to me, made a statement that has bothered me: "I knew if you came, Neil would come," or something to that effect. That is not the reason someone should present themselves as a believer.

I have some memories about your own experience in accepting Christ. We were attending Southside Baptist Church. I suppose you have your own memories of that church. The first would probably be of the building in old town Port Neches. It had once been the First Baptist Church.

Within a few years Southside had moved to a new building on Llano Street. It was there you grew into a young boy, who, like me, listened to a lot of sermons, Sunday school lessons, etc. There, another revival occurred with Brother Hughes from Huntsville, Texas. I knew him from my days at Alvin, Texas, back in the 50s.

Your experience differed from mine, and I can only relate it from my perspective. We returned home one night of the revival, and you had been touched by the sermon and worship. My memory tells me that you and I went into your small bedroom in our house on Goodwin Avenue. We talked and prayed, and you committed yourself to believe Jesus Christ as your savior.

You did not make the journey to present yourself to the church until a little later. Your mother and I were concerned about Southside, especially about you. There were no others of your age group attending. After talking and thinking about it, we decided to move our membership to the First Baptist Church, Port Neches. When we did, you accompanied us to the front and presented yourself as a believer for membership and for baptism.

All three of us had similar experiences under different circumstances, but I believe we all came to a peace of mind in our relationship to God. Whatever good thing God had for Winnie, she has gone to enjoy. I have been allowed a longer time with you and all our friends and family. Although you have chosen to embrace another faith group, I still marvel at the blessings God has given us together.

17 The Goose Hunting Lease

A few days ago, Carolyn and her two grandchildren visited me for five days. On Thursday of that visit, we wanted to treat the children to a day on the beach, so we took them to Galveston. This is not about that trip, except to say I learned to keep my shoes on to walk across the hot sand.

As we drove toward Galveston, I partially remembered a goose-hunting trip we had together. This must have occurred in your teenage years.

I had a lease to hunt on some acreage between Winnie and High Island. Ollie Miller and Percy Bourque were also on the lease. Ollie was into goose hunting in a big way, with many decoys, white sheets, goose calls, the whole nine yards. Percy was primarily interested in a place for his Beagle dogs to find and chase rabbits.

I had an incident with Percy that scared me as I had never been scared before. We had been to the lease on a Saturday morning and were returning on the highway between Winnie and Port Arthur. Percy was driving his pickup truck at a respectable speed. All at once he slumped over onto me, out like a light. It became a big concern for me because we were still cruising along with no hands on the steering wheel or foot on the brakes.

I managed to push Percy off so he leaned against the driver's door. Now I could get my hands on the steering wheel. I don't remember if his foot was still on the accelerator, but my main objective was to get my foot all the way over to the brake pedal. Finally, I guided the truck over to the side of the road and to a stop. By the time all this happened, Percy was waking up, or becoming conscious. Needless to say, I drove the remaining way home.

Back to our goose hunt: We had gone in the afternoon and, as usual, had no luck of killing a goose or anything. The day was coming to an end, and we were surprised as the geese either decided to come home or at least change fields.

Some of those birds came in so low that it seemed impossible we could not have killed our limit. I don't remember what gun you had, probably the 410 shotgun I had purchased for you. I believe we both fired as many rounds as we had in our guns. The resulting gunfire only brought down one lonely goose.

Now, all this happened close to sundown, and there was a time when shooting became illegal. We got that goose and loaded it into the vehicle as quickly as possible for the journey home.

As I remember, your mother was not overjoyed with the result of our hunt. I had never cleaned and prepared a goose before, and that became an experience. Seems a lot of a goose is down as well as feathers. This really cooled my desire for goose hunting. As I remember, Winnie cooked the goose later, and we "enjoyed" it.

The lease had other features that were more rewarding. Rusty was our dog at that time, and he dearly loved those fields, especially the small tallow trees and brush that grew along the ditches crossing the lease. Rusty had a good nose for quail. We had not trained him properly to hold a point, and he would point and then jump on the quail or into the covey.

Isn't it good to remember those persons and the anxiety of the hunt that was Rusty's?

18 Baby It's Cold Outside

In 1943, the average cost of a new house was $3,600; average wages per year, $2,000; average price for a new car, $900; cost of a gallon of gas, 15 cents; a bottle of Coca-Cola was 5 cents. Our house was more in the $700 range, including about half an acre of land. Our house was built in about 1905 and was single-wall construction with light gauze-like material tacked to the boards and then paper glued to it. This did not keep out a lot of the north wind.

Something else was taking place down at Malakoff's Kilman Hospital on January 7, 1943. A new baby boy, "Jimmie," had been born to the Duncan and Edith (Brown) Taliaferro family and was soon transported to the residence of the Brown grandparents. This is when it got really interesting.

Not long after the baby and his mother arrived and were assigned to a bedroom in the home, the weather began to worsen. By the next morning the temperature had dropped to around eight degrees, and all the heaters had ceased to burn.

We Browns were one of the few newly converted users of butane for heating and cooking. The butane storage tank was buried with only a lid-covered area showing. It contained the valves for filling and gauging as well as the piping connects leading under the house. The house was on piers, and the piping for heaters and the cookstove had not been put underground.

When the temperature nears or drops below freezing, butane returns to a liquid state. When the pipes were installed, they were not slanted back toward the tank. If properly installed, the liquid butane probably would have drained back to the tank; however, it just puddled in the lines, so no gas was reaching the heaters or the cookstove. That baby and new mother were going to get cold really quickly; the cold air seemed to pass right through those thin walls.

Duncan went off somewhere and came back with a coal-oil heater and set it up in the bedroom. Today, I continually wonder that all had not become asphyxiated by the fumes from the heater. Grandfather Homer just about froze his hands and body trying to drain the liquid butane from the lines. The two young uncles managed to get invited to a neighbor's house.

I imagine Jimmie may still get cold when the temperature goes below 50 or so. You might say he was greeted into the world on the cold side. Guess he has just shivered around for more than 70 years.

19 The Journey to Senior Buyer

As you know, I retired from Texaco Chemical Company in Port Neches, Texas, as a senior buyer. The route to that position ran a little rough and unscripted. Not many persons tell the company they want to leave a responsible job and are willing to leave the company in order to accomplish that end. I suppose God protects fools like that and had mercy on me to work a miracle through other persons. I'll try to relate it as I saw it.

During the 1970s the transportation supervisor for Texaco Chemical plant at Port Neches retired. This occurred during a strike situation at the plant. I had been a supervisor working directly under him for several years. I immediately assumed that responsibility. For several months I performed the two jobs. I don't know the cause of a lengthy delay, but I was eventually elevated to the position of transportation supervisor, and another person was assigned to my former position.

About a year later an incident occurred that made my usefulness and authority as a supervisor and leader in the transportation department seem meaningless. After a weekend of consultation with Winnie, I went to the superintendent under whom I worked and informed him that I wanted to be relieve of the job I now held and would consider any position the company might have anywhere in the world. If a place could not be arranged, I would consider leaving the company. I'll try to describe the situation as I saw it.

The day of the incident was a Friday. As I passed through the plant gate going to my office, one of the security guards informed me that a tank wagon for loading chemicals had been in the plant for several hours. Immediately upon arrival at my desk, I called the unit responsible for loading the carrier. They informed me the reason the carrier had not been loaded was that the inspection sheet containing information and loading instructions did not have one of the places checked. After determining what needed to be checked, I told them to check that place and load the carrier. The company had a customer awaiting the arrival of this product.

An hour or so later, the security guard called and again reminded me the tank wagon had not been loaded. I made a second call to the loading unit.

Later that morning, we had the daily staff meeting for all the supervisors to report to the superintendent. When it came my turn to speak, I began to broach the subject of the delay in the tank wagon being loaded in the early morning hours. The superintendent immediately cut off my report and informed the group this would be taken up later.

The meeting resumed, and all the others were heard. With the dismissal the superintendent requested the supervisors from the tank wagon loading unit and I remain. After the other persons had left the room, the superintendent retrieved a paper from his desk and scooted his chair across the room and held the paper in front of me.

He said, "You have to see the loading document instructions were not completely filled out, don't you?" (or something to that effect).

In my memory there was one item that had not been checked; I believe it had to do with the non-hazardous character of the chemical being loaded. I could hardly believe the superintendent's reaction. He had characterized me as inefficient and ineffective in front of all the supervisors in the room. What he had not taken into account was that all the supervisors had been schooled on the new loading instruction sheet just a few weeks before. The one on the shift could have checked the sheet and had the tank wagon loaded. The supervisors were well aware of the nature and character of the chemical being loaded.

Being criticized at that level and before my peer supervisors was demeaning. I left the room and thought about what had happened. I don't believe I felt anger. I had come through about eighteen months of stress and depression. I had taken my lunch, so I retrieved it and told the fellow who was second in command that I was leaving. I really did not know what to do. Finally, I got in my truck and drove over to the mall in Beaumont. I walked and then sat, allowing the day to pass.

Over the weekend Winnie and I discussed what had happened. I was especially concerned that my role as a supervisor had been destroyed. We decided I would go in on Monday and tell the superintendent I wanted to vacate the position. This was not easy as, after beginning work there, I had taken and passed additional traffic courses at Lamar in Beaumont.

After a few months went by, a position opened up at the plant, and it was offered to me. I didn't know how buying lingerie for dollar store would mesh with buying pipes and valves, but I would try.

This was some of the road to the senior buyer job, but this is not the important part. Winnie saw me through a very challenging time in the 70s, and you were a part of that. I have no way of knowing how much and to what degree it affected you as individuals, but I am eternally grateful to you. For an ending, though, God blessed me, and after an adjustment in knowing nomenclature for all the various items around a chemical plant, I had some of the best 10 or so years of my work experience.

Harold Brown Writes*

COUNTERACTION

Money Trees

Now, a money tree would come in very handy around most households and businesses I know. I never have been fortunate enough to acquire or even see one of those creations, but it seems that by popular thought, some individuals have come to the conclusion that good old Uncle Sam is just a big money tree.

I read somewhere once, "A dollar in the bush looks bigger than a dollar in the hand." I suppose this is a pretty logical assumption. We are pretty bad about seeing all those dollar marks superimposed upon the scraggly bushy beard and outreached limb of the good uncle, and our own miserly dollars seem inconsequential. We want our projects financed so we arouse our own pet political tree shaker, and off he goes to shake the money tree.

There are two things, possibly, we fail to take into consideration. First, we are going to have to give up more and more of our miserly small dollars to feed that tree. Even this money tree must have a steady diet to perform. If at any time it overbears and that tree shaker gathers the fruit, the intake of our dollars will have to increase to keep it strong and healthy.

The second consideration must be for the compensation of that tree shaker. If the tree shaker be politician or pressure group makes little difference. He is either going to become a party to the productivity of the tree, or he is going to be a participant in the food we contribute to the tree. Either way, our miserly dollars are going to suffer the consequences.

The more I think about this thing, the less I think about the goodness that comes from a money tree type of Uncle Sam. I wonder if it might be possible to picture the caricature once again to display honor, diplomacy, statesmanship, and courage.

20 The Senior Trip

It has been the custom of high schools to let those who have completed the required course of study to take a trip or have some special celebratory time together. A couple things are important about this: one, in small school systems it recognizes that many of the graduates have been classmates for a considerably long time; two, in all probability this will be the last time these students will be together as a group. So it was that we carried on a tradition.

The Malakoff High School graduating class of 1946, even though it was recognized as the twelfth grade of the school, actually had only been in the school system for 11 years. It was during this time that Texas schools added a year to make it a 12-year system. As I remember, we skipped eighth grade; how they worked this out is still a mystery to me.

After these 11 years what would be the proper way to celebrate and honor this group of students? There were the normal activities: prom (dinner, no dancing); baccalaureate; and graduation, where the diplomas would be passed out. As mentioned, some schools sponsored a getaway trip to places like Austin, the state capital, extending the school learning process, or to Galveston or Corpus Christi on the Gulf of Mexico. Some schools even scheduled trips to Washington or New York.

We did have our day! It was a bus ride to Tyler, the rose capital of the world, to a tent-covered skating rink. I think our class treasury was rather meager. Our town had not only survived the terrible depression and a world war but experienced the loss of their main enterprise, the coal mines. Texas Power and Light had converted their Trinidad generating plant to natural gas, and the lignite coal was no longer needed to fuel the plant.

My friend Joe and I had enjoyed a lot of activities together during our high school years, but I don't recall ever trying our hand at skating. In fact, I can hardly believe anyone in the class had a lot of time and experience on skates. Glover and R. J., along with a couple others, could have given us lessons on trying to ride a yearling calf, but neither, as I remember, had very much experience on roller skates. Bonnie, the pixie-like classmate from English and Spanish classes, who was very prim and easily embarrassed by just teasing, found a new meaning for the loss of demeanor when confronting a pair of roller skates.

Perhaps one of the reasons most of the class had not been accomplished on roller skates was the fact that our town had lost a lot of residents and was no longer attractive to the traveling skating rinks to come and set up for business. As the mines closed, there was an exodus of people, and as the wartime enterprises developed, they sought employment away from Malakoff. Airplane manufacturing in the Dallas/Fort Worth area attracted some. Others found their places in Houston or along the Gulf Coast for ship building or other wartime manufacturing. This caused the skating rink operators to bypass Malakoff for the larger towns and cities.

Another reason we did not learn to skate was the lack of sidewalks. Only one section of town had sidewalks, and I can think of no one in the senior class who lived in that area of town.

We did go skating, however, and we gave it our best shot. We had fun and created a memory of a special day commemorating years of togetherness for some of us. We recognized the special friends we had acquired as we sought our education, students as well as sponsors. A few of us carried away a scar or two, but we have never forgotten our senior trip.

21 The Wrong Runway

Although it was a rather short period of time (even though it didn't seem so then), enlisting and serving in the Air Force possibly influenced my life as much or more than any comparable time period. It gave me experiences that began to change me as an individual and give me insights beyond the small town in which I grew up. This does not diminish the life values instilled in the first 20 years.

When I enlisted in the Air Force, the last thing in my mind was the thought that I would be flying. Pilots do that! I had flown one time in a small aircraft, but that's another story. During World War II most of my experience with airplanes was lying on my back on a summer day watching the flyers from the air base in Corsicana do barrel rolls or loops in their blue and yellow airplanes. The Army Air Corps designation was PT-19 (open cockpit, one student pilot, and one instructor). This is one of the places young men were given their first flight training. On occasion we were visited by planes from Terrell. I think the flyers being trained there may have been from England. These were designated PT-17 and were biplanes, having an upper and lower wing, but with the blue and yellow colors.

Eighteen or so months after I enlisted, I found myself on flying status as a flying radar mechanic. This was so I could fly to diagnose problems occurring with radar when flying that did not happen when ground tested. I only had to fly about four hours a month to be paid the extra money, so I did not have to go up very often.

The airplanes assigned to my squadron were designated B-25 and were of World War II vintage. This airplane had been made famous early in the war by General Doolittle and the men he trained for a special mission. The government wanted to make a statement to the Japanese. What better way than to attack the homeland of Japan? We did not have planes with the range to reach Japan and return to a safe landing. A plan was devised for transporting planes by aircraft carrier close to Japan, launching the planes, and letting them proceed to unoccupied China after their bombing was complete.

The B-25 was chosen for this, and General Doolittle set about training chosen flyers to be able to take off these planes, loaded to capacity, in the length of an aircraft carrier. I looked up some things that probably helped in choosing this plane: bomb capacity: 2,400 pounds; 1,200-mile range; and 300 MPH. The mission was accomplished, and the B-25 became famous. You can find the story in the film *Thirty Seconds over Tokyo*.

I told you all this to acquaint you with the pilots who were assigned to fly our missions out of Ellington. Most of the pilots had come to us from twin-engine flight training school. They all knew the story and I am sure had seen the movie about Doolittle and his boys. The short takeoff was intriguing. I think it never occurred to them they had a rather large radome attached underneath the planes we used. They knew, however, the flying speed they needed to reach for safe takeoff.

A takeoff could be, at times, like this. The plane would taxi in the takeoff line, and when its turn came for takeoff, the plane would be aligned on the runway. The brakes would be locked, everything checked, and the throttles shelved forward until the engines were at full power; it felt like every rivet was ready to pop. Then the brakes released, and that plane would jump forward. It was an exhilarating experience as the plane lifted off the runway as flying speed was reached. Oh, what fun! The flight would soon become leisurely as cruising altitude was reached.

The B-25 has a small tunnel under the left side of the pilot's compartment. This provides entrance into the Plexiglas greenhouse of the plane's far-ward end. In combat this would be the position of the bombardier. Once reached, the greenhouse provides a view and an isolation from the world. Occasionally, the quietness may be broken by a comment over the headset.

Twilight from 10,000 feet is different than that experienced at ground level. The plane is surrounded by the bright sunlight with reflections from the clouds, but nearly two miles below the darkness has begun to sweep across the countryside, only interrupted by tiny single lights with occasional clusters of lights denoting a town or city.

After some four hours the radio intersection has been reached and the descent begun, and the darkness below has given way to the many lights of the city of Houston. I-45 has made its track across the city and ends at Park Place. The plane is now aligning with two rows of lights outlining the runway.

The Plexiglas compartment is abandoned, and seating is made behind the two pilots in preparation for landing. The interphone crackles to life, and at once the engines regain their driving force, clawing for altitude. The pilots have realized the runway lights are not that of Ellington Field but rather the big Houston airport. The props bite into the night air, and correction is made for approach to Ellington.

What was experienced in those few minutes is somewhat life-like. Things we choose to guide us along in our life are attractive and alluring but lead toward the wrong goals and aspirations. We must make decisions for correction toward the real needs and benefits of life.

22 The Three 'Amigos'

In September 1935 three youngsters made their way to Alamo Ward Grammar School in Malakoff to begin first grade. Miss Emma Laura Evans greeted Roy Weldon Martin, Roger Wayne Evans, and Homer Harold Brown along with others.

As the quote goes, "It was the best of times; it was the worst of times." Malakoff was a bustling East Texas community, including Kilman Hospital, *Malakoff News*, Kirby's Grocery and Dry Goods, Harbour's Grocery, Hugh Drane Ice Plant, Gulf Market, Royall Chevrolet Company, Carson Lumber Company, and Malakoff Fuel Company. These businesses provided jobs and services to the wide area of Malakoff and its surrounding territory. Residents worshiped at First Baptist Church, First Methodist Church, Assembly of God, Church of Christ, and a Catholic church that served the Mexican miners' families.

Farm prices were low, and cattle had to be slaughtered to reduce production so prices would rise. There was no social security, disability payments, or unemployment payments. Unemployed persons, widows, and orphans depended on family and community organizations for help.

The three boys were schooled together and were churched together until two dreadful things happened affecting the people of Malakoff. First, the Malakoff Fuel Company ceased operation. Second, pre-world war unrest was stirring the country. Roger's father was in the Army reserves.

The trio's common school experience included teachers like Miss Cally Johnson, Miss Edna Willis, Miss Nell Jarvis, Miss Annie Pope Gilreath, and Mr. W. T. Davis. The three attended First Baptist Church and were pastored by Brother J. L Brantley and at times Brother Stanley Wilkes. Sunday school teachers like Mrs. Cooper Reese and Mrs. Louis Scholl contributed to the religious training. Another aspect of worship was the music or song service led by Mr. Finis Hardy, who was accompanied by Mrs. Dorothy Hardy.

When the Malakoff Fuel Company ceased operation, both of my friends' fathers found themselves unemployed. Roy's father was either the fireman or engineer for the railroad engine operated by the fuel company. Each day, train loads of coal were transported to the Texas Power and Light Company's generating plant at Trinidad. Mr. Martin found employment in Needles, California, and proceeded to move his family there. The family's relatives were left in the community, and Roy's grandfather became a good reason for him to visit and keep our friendship alive.

Roger's father was faced with a different problem. He was an accountant for the fuel company, but the determining factor in leaving Malakoff was very different. Mr. Evans had been a member of the Reserve Officers Training Corp

(ROTC) in college. Prior to World War II the government called to active duty National Guard and reserve officers. Mr. Evans was called to active duty, and the family moved to Lawton, Oklahoma. Roger's Grandmother Evans and Mrs. Opal Evans' mother and father gave him reason to visit and keep our friendship alive.

Since I was the only one who remained in Malakoff, it was my good fortune to be able to greet and have time with Roy and Roger as they returned to visit. All three of us finished high school in various places and started very different life tracks. However, unbeknownst to one another, we all ended up in the U.S. Air Force.

Roy was the first to enlist in the Air Force in 1947. After completion of basic training, Roy attended radio school and was assigned to headquarters of the 15th Air Force in Colorado Springs. He completed his enlistment there.

I was the second to enlist in 1948 and after basic training was selected for radar school in Biloxi, Mississippi. After completion of the school, I was assigned to the 3605th navigator training wing at Ellington Air Force Base in Houston. I completed my enlistment there, plus one additional year (for a total of four years) because of the Korean conflict.

Roger was the last to enter the Air Force. He soon found himself in pilot training and upon completion was chosen for single-engine jet training. The F-86 became his vehicle, and he earned a place on a team that demonstrated jet-fighter capability for air shows around the United States.

On Sunday, May 13, 2001, the three of us reunited for the first time since 1946. Since I lived in Malakoff until leaving for the Air Force, I had met each of my friends at various times as they would visit their relatives. This time, however, we were all together, joined by our wives: Barbara (Roy), Shirley (Roger), and of course Winnie. As Roy, Roger, and I recalled old times and shared life experiences, we found that 70-plus years of life had not dulled our expectations for tomorrow.

Some of the writing for this story was taken from an article I wrote that was published in the *Malakoff News*. Over the years the *News* published articles and letters to the editor I had written. I am grateful for the privilege of being published and especially for Louis Scholl, long-time editor and publisher of the *News*.

23 Leaves, Leaves

Each fall, usually in October, nature begins to redress the countryside. It may be that God checks his inventory of the reds, golds, maroons, and browns in nature's storehouse of colors. He tells his angel painters to use them before the cold winds and icy rain comes to detract man's thoughts.

In our country it begins in the far reaches of Maine and slowly spreads over the New England states: Vermont, New Hampshire, Connecticut, New York, etc. The bright sun shining full on a mountainside sets the maple trees aflame from the valley to the highest peak.

I believe it was the first fall after Winnie retired in 1982 that we "had to go see the leaves." We found a bus tour company in Arlington, Texas, that seemed to meet our needs. The company had been founded by a former Baptist education minister. He had first planned trips for the church he served, and the trips gained such popularity that others came to have him plan for them. Soon, he formed company, which had grown rather large. Our "leaf trip" was routed through New York City, and we stayed at the Plaza Hotel. We were told that during that fall's leaf time, the company had scheduled 40 bus loads to stay at the Plaza. The tour company owner's mother and father were there at the hotel to greet us travelers.

After the northeastern states have received their color, it spreads to Pennsylvania and West Virginia. The hills and dales of Virginia, Kentucky, the Carolinas, and Tennessee become endless color. A memorable view was the Blue Ridge Parkway of western North Carolina.

Later, Winnie and I came to seek out special fall foliage tours mostly by our car. Arkansas brings to mind a drive up Highway 7 (goes through Booger Hollow) and the Ouachita, Burton, and Ozark Mountains.

Another bus trip found us seeking the golden aspen of Colorado. "Thar's gold in them there hills" was the theme as we traveled west to venture into the Tetons and up to Yellowstone, where a soft snowfall greeted us as an accent to the color.

I would be remiss if I did not remind that here in the Golden Triangle along about the middle of November, God's angels use up the remaining inventory of colors to cloak the tallow trees with a "coat of many colors."

24 Steak House Sign

Carolyn has come back into our lives more lately than she has been for some time. Our acquaintance and love for her goes back into the early 1960s. She and her then-husband, Forrest, came to Port Neches—he to teach at the Port Neches Middle School, the same school in which Winnie was teaching; she to begin her lifelong career of teaching piano.

After a short time Forrest and Winnie became acquainted at school, and Forrest suggested to Carolyn that she meet Winnie. I don't remember the first meeting of the families, but before long the five of us would enjoy a Friday or Saturday night outing at a restaurant in the area. This usually meant a trip to Port Arthur or Beaumont because there were not many good restaurants in mid-county.

Carolyn likes to relate some of the things we did to illustrate our long friendship. This is one she and I have used and one you no doubt remember.

The five of us had made our way to a steakhouse in Beaumont for an outing at the end of a week. In my memory it was located somewhere on the circle that was adjacent to the Baptist hospital. We had arrived at the restaurant and placed our orders when you decided you needed to go to the restroom. This was a pretty nice restaurant in which we had chosen to dine. As I remember, Winnie had dressed you rather well for a four- or five-year-old.

We made a spur-of-the-moment decision that you could go alone. Off you went, your little head bobbing up and down as you made your way hurriedly through the tables toward the restroom.

It seemed like no time until the four of us began to see your little head bobbing up and down as you made your way back toward the table. I don't know if it had crossed our minds how quickly you had made the restroom trip, but that was answered rather quickly.

You came up to the table and presented yourself as one frustrated young lad. With no chance to question or comment, you announced, "You know I can't read!" This alerted Winnie and I into our places as parents.

This is a good memory for Carolyn and me. One of the things that comes to my mind as the years have passed is that this kind of freedom cannot be enjoyed by couples today. All the TV and news reports of children being taken and abused have made it a thing of the past, along with other freedoms children were once allowed. You gave us a good memory to relate when needed.

25 The Centennial

I have visited the Dallas/Fort Worth area quite a few times. I don't remember all the details about my first trip to Dallas, but a couple things were memorable.

The family visited Dallas in 1936. The occasion was "Centennial," a celebration of Texas's 100-year anniversary. I believe my brother Robbie took us in his '35 Ford two-door sedan, which he purchased new. It became the family means of transportation for a long time.

I am sure we were among the most googly-eyed of all the people at the celebration. One of the displays that has remained with me over the years was a main street attraction. As you know, companies sometimes use animals as part of their logos or in their advertising. The gecko lizard is one we are familiar with, and the Mobil Oil Company for years used a flying red horse. The one that made a high impression on me was the one Sinclair Oil Company used—a brachiosaurus. Sinclair's colors were green and black, and the dinosaur appeared on their oil cans, gasoline pumps, other products, and advertising.

As we made our way down the main street of the fair, what greeted us was a sight to behold. There on one of the corners was a Sinclair service station, and hovering over it was this huge green dinosaur. I may be wrong, but I believe it was animated so the long neck and small head moved slowly from side to side. What a sight!

Another thing that comes to my memory was the visit to the aquarium. There was one tank in that aquarium that really impressed me with an enormous catfish leisurely swimming around. As I remember, it weighed over 100 pounds. Seems the information may have indicated it was from the Missouri or Mississippi River.

Grandmamma Brown liked to fish about as much as anyone in this world. In later years I believe she may have carried a fishing line and bobber in her purse. Daddy would not have been very excited by it because he did not take to fishing too much. We really had a good family dinner if Grandmamma Brown or Brother Robbie had good luck fishing. To see that much fish swimming around just seemed to embed itself in my memory.

I used to love to fish a little myself, but I was never much of a catcher. I finally came to the mind that instead of finding all the gear to fish and taking the time to get to the place to fish, I could easily get in my automobile and drive to the local catfish restaurant and eat to my desire.

Why I remember such details, I really don't know. The mind seems to have little hidden places where the most inane things are stored.

26 Grandmamma's Week

Grandmamma Brown never did weigh over a hundred pounds. She had mental health problems in the 40s and had to be treated in a sanitarium in Dallas. She kept our home during the 30s and 40s by hard work and a lot of faith. Her days and weeks were full of task and caring. I'll try to describe a little and reflect on how much she provided for our family.

With which day should I begin? I suppose Monday would be as good as any, keeping in mind every day had common needs that were supplied by the family mother.

The day started early. Breakfast had to be prepared so the man of the house could arrive at work by 8:00 or 8:30. Since my father was a carpenter, his job locations changed, so his travel time varied. We children had to be fed and checked for dress, hair combed, and off to walk to school by 8:00 or 8:30. In addition to the breakfast preparation, Dad had milked the cow, and the milk had to be strained and placed in the ice box. Milk from the day before had cream accumulate on the surface, so that had to be skimmed for churning.

Churning did not happen every day. Several days' skimming would be churned at varied times of the week. At times we had more milk than we could use, so that was sold and delivered along with excess butter from the churning.

If it was not rainy or extremely cold, Dad had a fire going under the wash pot outside and filled it with water and soap (sometimes the soap would be lye soap made from the fatty cooking of a slaughtered hog). The white clothes—sheets, pillowcases, shirts, underwear, and the like—would be boiled first.

Colored clothes would follow after the whites had been removed to the rinse waters. The last boiling would usually contain Dad's work clothes and our school clothes.

After the clothes were boiled in the wash pot, there were normally three wash tubs sitting on a bench; each had its special use. The first tub (which would sometimes contain heated water) was the scrub tub. If the clothes had dirty spots, additional soap would be applied and the scrub board used to rub the soap item until it was clean. The next tub was the first rinse, and the clothes were worked to get as much soap out as possible. Then each item would be wrung out and passed on to the final tub, where "Mrs. Steward's Bluing" (a concentrated liquid that added a blue tint to the white clothes) had been added to the water. White cloth has a tendency to yellow as it ages; "bluing" counteracts yellowing. All the clothes went through the three waters for a scrubbing and two rinses. After the clothes had been washed, they were taken to the clothesline to hang and dry. When dried in the sun, the white clothes would be snow white.

This made for a heavy workload on washday. However, between the stirring, scrubbing, and hanging, there was preparation for a noon meal and an afternoon meal. This was a hard way to start a week for a frail housewife.

Tuesday morning came quickly! Remembering that breakfast preparation happens every day and yesterday was spent washing and drying clothes, it takes little to surmise that Tuesday was ironing day. Some of the clothes required a sprinkle of water as they were ironed. We had some old cast-iron irons that were used primarily as doorstops. These were from an earlier age when they had to be heated on a stove or in the fireplace (note about cast-iron irons: usually the ironing person would have two irons; one would be placed on or in the heat source, and then they were alternated). My mother did have an electric iron. Along with the sprinkling, some clothes required starch. The starch was added to water and the clothes dipped in the solution. When ironed, the starched clothes became rather stiff, but stiff collars were in vogue.

Someone might have had to do a little churning when everything quieted down in the evening.

Wednesday, some outside-the-home activities became a part of Mamma's week. Maybe the Woman's Missionary Union (WMU) would meet to discuss missions programs or activities. She had to walk to the church or to the home where the WMU circle met. During part of the time, Mamma was the leader of the "cradle roll department" of the First Baptist Church, and she thought that it was her duty to enroll every baby that was born to church members as soon as possible. I remember one time she walked out to the Drake home to enroll a one- or two-day-old baby. The Drakes lived outside town about a mile from our house.

For a while Grandmamma was the leader of the Royal Ambassadors, a group Baptists formed in place of the Boy Scouts. Of course, with her as the leader, there were no campouts or outside activities; it was mostly Bible and missions studies. Wednesday was also the day for the midweek prayer service at church.

Thursday was house-cleaning day. It began with a complete sweeping of the floors. After the sweeping came the mopping, which was sufficient for the linoleum, but the wood floors required the application of a light oil to pick up all the dust. We did not have carpet or large woven rugs, but we did have small rugs that had to be taken outside and beaten to remove any accumulated dirt and sand.

Friday had come too soon, and thoughts were turned to the weekend. Grandmamma would wash and set her hair in the home. I can remember Grandmamma using homemade curlers. Coffee cans at that time were opened by using a key. A small tab on the side of the can was inserted into the slot in the key and the key turned so as to cause a quarter-inch ribbon of tin to be pulled from the side of the can. After the can was opened, the thin ribbon of tin could be unrolled and cut into various lengths. Strips of cloth were then wrapped around the tin strips to cover the sharp edges. Various lengths of the tin strips could be used to roll the damp hair. The ends of the tin strips were bent to keep them from unrolling as the hair dried.

Friday was also a day that could be used for darning and mending. Just because a sock appeared with a hole in the toe or heel did not mean it was discarded. Sometimes a used light bulb had been kept for just such a time. The light bulb could be inserted into the sock, toe or heel, and it made a perfect way to use a needle and thread to bind up the hole in the sock. Mending also might be called for if one of us had torn a hole in the knee of our jeans. Old jeans and overalls were kept to use as patching material. One time, the entire lower front, from the knee down, of the leg of my overalls was replaced by a big patch. Don't remember how I tore that much material, but it could have been that I crawled through a barbed-wire fence in too big a hurry.

Friday could have meant a lot of other things: bed clothes mended, potted plants tended, quilting, crotchet work, dress or shirt sewing, and we always had a big garden.

Grandmamma's Saturdays were a little different to begin with because, except for my oldest brother having to go to work, the rest of us had a changed day schedule. Daddy did not normally work away from home on Saturday. Garden work and the normal tending of the cow and chickens had to be done. Saturday shopping for the necessities we could not grow or raise had to be done. Saturday was also catch-up day for anything we had missed during the week—for instance, if the churning had not been done, or milk and butter not delivered, or a visit not made.

For a lot of kids, Saturday meant a Saturday afternoon Western, but my brother and I did not get to attend many of these. Movies were thought to be instruments of the devil by some, and that is where my folks came down in their system. We had the same heroes by radio: Lone Ranger, Hopalong Cassidy, Tom Mix, plus Little Orphan Annie.

Sunday, the day of rest! Well, the cow had to be milked and the chickens fed and breakfast prepared with the thought in mind that by 9:00 or 9:30 it would be Sunday school time. If the Saturday night bath had been missed by someone, it had to happen. Worship at church would begin at 11:00, and the length of the service had to do with minister's sermon length and how many verses of the invitation were sung.

The family dinner was served as quickly as possible upon arrival home from church. Usually, Saturday and Sunday morning preparation made possible a fairly quick mealtime. The exception was when the preacher came to dinner or we had company for dinner. This usually took longer because cooking such dinners as fried chicken took longer to prepare because Grandmamma would always want it to be hot and the biscuits fresh out of the oven.

Sunday evening could be a quiet time for Grandmamma, I suppose. She thought it not proper to work on Sunday. On occasions we might go and visit relatives or friends, but such visits were rare. Of course, by sundown it would be time to go to church again for the evening activities of training and worship service.

This has been a sampling of Grandmamma's week. I think to some extent all the Grandmammas of the 30s and early 40s in East Texas had similar schedules because there were few machines and instruments in those days to do a lot of things that occurred around a home. If a family had sufficient income, some of the things Grandmamma did would have been done by outside help. A lot of families were like mine. Theirs was a hand-to-mouth existence of difficult work.

27 My Earliest Memory

Have you ever tried to recall your earliest memory? When we old people start recalling happenings from our younger days, we think we want to revert to such a time. Sometimes our memories remind us how fortunate we have been to have lived through some really good times, especially the economic and technological advances we have enjoyed.

The earliest memories I seem to recall must have occurred when I was two or three years old. I remember being out by the fireplace chimney and becoming aware of the moon. It was in the daylight hours, and the full moon was visible faintly against the blue sky. I guess I had never seen this before, and it seemed no matter which side of the chimney I looked up, I could see this moon. I hurried inside to tell Mama. No other details come to mind. As I think back on it, I guess God shows his wonders to all the world, even to a little toddler.

While we were living at this place, which was south of Malakoff and up a country lane and then a long driveway up a slight hill, there was another happening. This one involved my old brother, Robbie, and Daddy. Some of this I did not observe but remember because of the consequences.

Robbie, who was still in high school, had been called to help Daddy catch and harness the mules. I don't remember what the mules were being caught for, but I believe Daddy had or was trying to raise some cotton. The mules must have been a little skittish.

There was a mule chase that ensued with Daddy being the mule chaser and Robbie the one to head the mules off or corner them. There must have been some frustration on Robbie's part. Somewhere along the chase, he had picked up a brick, which he let fly as the mules rounded the barn. The mules were faster than Daddy, and the brick hit him in the head.

What I have told you thus far I did not observe, but I do remember Daddy being in the house and Dr. Kilman coming to see him. I suppose today we would say he had a concussion. I don't remember any other details, but maybe it was told as a humorous incident after Daddy recovered. Later, Daddy had a mental problem that I think did not have anything to do with this incident, but that is another story that had a more life-changing outcome.

This story illustrates the struggles Daddy seemed to have in his lifelong experiences, but it also marks the first time I became aware of how Robbie was to be a helper and sometimes provider for the family. I probably never expressed the thanks he deserved as an older brother.

28 The Rose Parade

Music has always been interesting to me. Of course, in elementary school and at church we had times to sing along with other people, and there were times when I listened as other persons performed. My first official music training began when I was in eighth grade.

I don't remember how we obtained the trumpet. Mr. Russ, the high school band director, probably helped us find it. Then he began to teach me the little things you have to know about playing a musical instrument—how to hold my mouth and lips, even my tongue! Then there was this thing about those three valves that were operated by proper fingering. I still wonder at the patience of music teachers.

The story I want to tell is not about my musical ability. School had not been in session very long when I received an invitation to go with the band to Tyler for the Rose Parade. Mr. Russ needed a person to fill out his marching formation, and even though I was inexperienced, I was asked to be that one. Mr. Russ had found a uniform that would fit me, and prior to going we had marching practice. I was to march on the right side of the band and in the last rank or line. I was given instruction that when the band played during the parade, I was to hold the trumpet up to my lips like I was playing.

We rode a bus over to Tyler on the given day for the parade, and I came to think we were in rather "high cotton." Next to us when we lined up for the parade was a band from Southern Methodist University. Five or six weeks into learning to play the trumpet, I was marching with the best! I was a bit scared by this time.

It came time to join the marching line. I was instructed and had practiced guiding to the left to retain a straight line. I was to guide on John Melvin, probably a senior that year, who played the trumpet or cornet. Away we went!

The band proceeded down the cleared streets of Tyler, occasionally striking up a lively tune. I faked my playing with the best of them. I believe it was when the band entered the downtown square when it happened—John Melvin disappeared as my guide. I glanced back as he regained his footing and raced to catch up. A lot of town squares (usually the courthouse was in the center of the square) had a little stop sign in the middle of the street as you entered the square. John Melvin had not seen the sign because we were in the last row, and he tripped over it.

One other time I remember a similar incident happening to a member of our band was at a parade in Athens. The parade had formed up around the high school and proceeded to the street that came into Athens from Jacksonville. There was one of those stop signs in the middle of the street at the entrance to the square.

Reagan was the band's bass drummer. He was about two years behind me at school and had inherited the job even though he had not reached his full height. The drummers took up about three lines in the back of the marching formation. I really don't think that made a difference; Reagan simply could not see over the big drum too well and tripped over the sign. However, he did not fall as John Melvin had done. Rather, he found himself draped over the drum. To the best of my knowledge, he never missed a beat. He rolled back to his feet, and the band played on.

I believe most of the stop signs have now been removed from the courthouse squares around East Texas, so band marchers are not faced with this problem now. I am grateful for the trust Mr. Russ placed in me as a beginning trumpet player. Watch out, Harry James!

29 It Was George

I am going to write about a person you may or may not remember. His name was George, and he came to Port Neches in the 60s (more about that visit later).

I believe George is one of the most interesting persons I have ever been privileged to know in my lifetime. I think it was because he was not just one person but a whole series of persons in one body. I guess you could call him a "chameleon."

When I first met and began to know about George, Winnie and I were in the early stage of courtship and marriage. George was married to Winnie's Aunt Merle, and I think we probably visited them in Houston very early in our relationship. Winnie would sometimes go to Houston during the summertime to fill in for Merle while she was on vacation or away on business. Merle had several Merle Norman cosmetic stores around the Houston area.

As I remember, George was working as a television salesperson at the time. The company George worked for was one of the leading sellers of televisions in the Houston area. George was not satisfied to be just a good salesperson but learned how to do minor repairs and respond to problem calls from his costumers. Television was new, and repair persons were few. George became involved in any endeavor he set out to do.

I learned a little about George as we visited and listened to stories of his early life. If I remember correctly, he did not finish high school, and he was raised in Chicago. He left there at a young age and began working as a seaman. The stories were that he worked his way through various marine skills and job requirements to hold three maritime licenses. It seems when he reached a certain level of excellence, it became a challenge to start over in a different field of endeavor. I suppose this was the first inkling to me that he was chameleon-like. As time went by, this was born out by his actions and lifestyle.

After I came to know about George, we heard he had quit his job in television sales and was working for a rather small store that sold fishing and watersports equipment in a shopping area not for from their home. It wasn't long before scuba diving, which I believe was just becoming popular as a watersport, emerged as his primary interest.

Soon, a swimming pool appeared in the family's backyard. If you are going to sell scuba-diving gear, you must have a place to demonstrate the equipment and give instruction on how to use it properly. Not long after that, George began escorting people who had purchased the equipment to the Gulf of Mexico for offshore diving.

Then, one day, a picture appeared in one of the Houston newspapers with a 600- or 700-pound jewfish. Beside it stood George with his spear gun. He was outsized by the fish. This seemed to lead to the next adventure.

After the picture appeared, George got or sought out a deal with one of the newspapers in Houston to do a column on scuba diving, spear fishing, and all the finer points of the sport. Now, it did not bother him that he didn't have a whole lot of education or writing experience. He simply scrolled out his column and gave it to Merle to edit and type for sending to the paper. I remember this as a weekly column.

George had made such a success out of the scuba diving that a major company in that business came to him to be their representative. I don't remember his exact territory, but I believe it covered Texas, Louisiana, and Mississippi. George didn't let this interfere with his newspaper writing. If he was on the road, he would either scratch out or dictate the writing and call in a stenographer to edit and type for submission. George was at the top of his game. I don't remember how long the scuba diving and column writing lasted.

At some point George became disinterested in the scuba diving. Winnie and I were not aware of what his interest might be until one day a while later. I learned it one day when I came home from work and a big black automobile was parked in front of our Combs Drive house. I learned George had appeared at Winnie's school to greet her when school was out. He was dressed to the nines, suit and tie, standing by his big black auto. I don't remember if it was a Lincoln or Cadillac.

George was now an insurance salesman. I think I'm still paying for a policy! He had become acquainted with a person who was building a rather new insurance company in Houston. The man was a Christian and was building the company on those principles. We learned later that George had begun attending church, and I believe he joined. He became what the businessman wanted as a representative of the company. Before long George was charged with opening up East Texas, and I believe he was assigned in the development of Oklahoma.

George had come a long way—from a sun-tanned, wind-burned man in scuba gear with a fishing spear to a white collar with tie and dark suit driving a long black car. He had made a transition.

Merle died rather unexpectedly in the late 1960s, and our relationship was very sketchy. Winnie's cousins let us know he had sold the Merle Norman studios Merle had operated and moved to Galveston.

Winnie and I (I don't remember if you were with us) were in Galveston sometime later. I believe someone had informed Winnie of the location of George's business in Galveston. On the eastern end of Galveston Island is a pier or seawall that is the favorite fishing place for many in Galveston. We drove down to where the pier joins the island, and there it was—a fishing bait stand with all the other fishing needs and the proprietor, George. You would have sworn you were being greeted by Ernest Hemingway: sun-tanned on every part of his swimsuit-exposed body; a scraggly beard that was beginning to gray and a sailor's cap tilted back on his head. He was the captain of his ship! We were graciously received as always.

As before, the news of George was sketchy, but we learned he had departed from Galveston and gone to Belize, a small coastal country in Central America. It is my understanding he was promoting a facility for travelers and vacationers from the States. Belize is an English-speaking country, but I can imagine George being able to speak the Spanish of the natives before long. I'm sure he had assumed whatever role was required to serve his needs and that of his clientele. Again, it is my understanding that after some time, he returned to the States and lived in New Orleans until his death.

I have been fortunate to have known some interesting persons: a Spanish-American War veteran, some World War I and World War II veterans, a bevy of persons holdings doctorate degrees for various professions, and a Holocaust survivor. I can think of none as colorful as George. He was truly a human chameleon.

Harold Brown Writes*

COUNTERACTION

The Fourth Branch of Government

The formal makeup of our government in America, as taught by the social science departments of our schools and colleges, encompasses three branches: legislative, executive, and judicial. There is one neglected branch that is more important than any one or a combination of the other three. The citizen branch of the government is, I believe, the most important.

The legislative branch of government is to reflect the will of the citizens of our republic. These reflections come to a climax in the statute books of the land. If we are neglectful in our duties as citizens, these laws of the land will not reflect the will of the people but may tend to subjugate the people to the wishes of the legislative body.

The executive branch of our government is deemed necessary to carry out the enforcement of the statutory decrees enacted by the legislative branch. There is no primary intent of the executive branch becoming an all-powerful, ruling personage. If the executive branch is to acclaim the right of statutory decree or the use of power politics to bring about its own wishes, our representative form of government will decay into anarchy.

The judicial branch of government is the interpreter of our statues. Basically, the judicial of government is to place within the framework of our Constitution a legal instrument of law.

What about the fourth branch? The citizens branch of government must clearly state its wishes as to the political atmosphere in which it wishes to dwell. If the morals and ethics of the fourth branch are to be reflected in the government of our land, we must rise up and assume our rightful position. If the citizens branch of government fails, we can only hope for chaos.

30 The Fire Phone

I was fortunate to go back to college after Winnie and I were married to earn a degree in business administration. This was not my intention when I decided to go back at the age of 30. I was going to try to work to earn a degree in religious education, but that changed after I entered the University of Corpus Christi (that's another story).

Upon graduating from UCC in August 1960, I was employed by Jefferson Chemical at the Port Neches plant as a clerk in shipping and receiving. The incident I am writing about occurred about 18 years later. I had been fortunate to be promoted to a position that when the plant traffic supervisor retired, I was assigned to that position. This happened when a strike had occurred at the plant.

One day as I sat in the traffic supervisor's office, the fire phone rang. Even though there was a plant-wide strike and most of the employees were away, there was a provision for firemen to answer any fire emergency. The information on the fire phone message indicated the emergency was close to the relatively new propane storage tanks. This was located just west of the traffic office building. A street ran alongside but about 30 yards away from the building.

My office window looked out toward the street the firefighting vehicles and personnel had to use to get to the emergency location. Not long after the fire phone message was completed, I viewed the plant fire truck as it passed down the street with those who had been assigned as firefighters and worked close enough to the fire house to clamber on the truck as it left. They were clinging to the truck.

Every firefighter was not that lucky. A few vehicles followed, and then along came those who were madly pedaling their bicycles. Lastly, there were a few stragglers on foot. Like a parade they passed and disappeared toward the emergency site.

I continued to work, assuming the emergency would be taken care of and that someone would call to advise us of any additional safety information. A few minutes later, I viewed out of my window a sight that bewildered me. I saw the fire truck coming down a street that paralleled the railroad yard to the south of the street it had traveled a short time ago. I realized the truck and the parade that followed had made a block and were coming back to a place they had already traveled. I assumed they had bypassed whatever emergency had occurred. What played out in my sight was like a *Laurel and Hardy* movie short.

I do not know what occurred as the firemen traveled to the emergency, but since there was no other call to advise of danger, I believed I was safe.

I do not tell this story to denigrate the fire brigade of the company. I know those who served in that capacity did so to the best of their ability and for the safety of the plant and its employees.

31 The Horse Ride

Carolyn has recently come back into a close relationship with us. She first came into our lives in the 1960s when she and her husband came to Port Neches. She and I have shared a story that recalls an early incident involving you. We like it, I think, because it reminds the two of us how long our friendship and caring for each other has existed.

Winnie was in the hospital in Beaumont when you were about four or five years old. I had determined to visit her on a Sunday afternoon and arranged for you to stay with Carolyn and Forrest. They wanted to give you a ride in the countryside and eventually stop at the home of another teacher from the middle school.

Sometime during the visit there, the friend showed you his horse. Now, can anyone think of a better experience for a youngster to have than to ride a very gentle horse? Everything went fine, and you got settled in the saddle. I don't know that anyone determined what caused the next thing to happen, but the horse began to pitch, and you became airborne. What goes up must come down, and you came down rather hard.

Sometime later, Carolyn arrived at the Baptist Hospital in Beaumont. She was very upset when she had to tell her bed-ridden friend that her son was in the emergency room with a broken collarbone. Carolyn still relates that Winnie, although concerned about you, began to console her and impress upon her that everything was going to be okay.

And it did work out okay. You got to stay out of school a few days, which made you happy because you got to stay with Carolyn. You also got a lifelong way to remind Carolyn of that Sunday afternoon horse ride. When you see her, you can simply point to your collarbone and grin with no comment.

32 Back to College

Life has led me to go places and do things I could never have dreamed of as child. One of the "doing things" happened in 1958. Winnie and I had settled down in La Porte, Texas. She had found a place to teach, and I had become the manager of a new variety store. We had found a church home in the community that accepted our presence and challenged us, especially me.

During the early part of the year, I began to question my life's aspirations. The church we attended was somewhat fundamental, and the pastor was very evangelical in his leadership. I cannot say how much that played into a decision Winnie and I came to embrace. We made the decision that I might look for or find a way to go back to college. I had credit for about a year and a half and wanted to go into the field of religious education.

One of the deciding factors occurred as we were dealing with making a firm decision. We traveled to Corpus Christi to visit Mom and Pop Harris and the rest of the family. There was a Baptist university in the city, and we visited it. Winnie determined she knew a person; I believe he was a principal in the Flour Bluff school district, a district lying just out of Corpus near the naval base. She decided to call him to determine if there might be possibility of finding a teaching job there. When she talked to him, he insisted that she come out and he would get her a meeting with the superintendent. She didn't want to go out at this time because she had not brought with us dress clothes proper for such a meeting. He insisted. She went, and when she returned, she reported she had a job for the following year.

I gave the store owners notice that I would be leaving to go back to college in September. This would allow them time to find a replacement for the La Porte store. The company had decided and was planning to open a store in Dickinson during summer. They arranged for a manager to take over the store in La Porte, and I was to oversee the laying out and stocking of the Dickinson store.

When school was out, Winnie joined me in the preparation for the grand opening of the new store. It turned out to be the biggest and best store opening the company had ever experienced. That first day, the citizens of Dickinson had lined up outside before the store opened. During the day it was so crowded that the customers could hardly make it up and down the aisles, especially with arms full of items to purchase. The registers would get so full, the drawers were difficult to close. Once or twice during the day, I would take the bills out of the register, place them in bank bags, and hide the bags.

I had a problem the next morning when we were making up the bank deposits. We came up rather short of what the register's read indicated. I think the general manager almost had a heart attack! I forgot to find one of the hiding places for the bags. A little searching solved the problem. This would have been my store, and we decided to walk away for hopefully a higher calling.

Since I had completed about a year and a half in college and the university gave me credit for the radar training in the Air Force, I was a junior religious education major. I began to act in that capacity at a church in Corpus Christi. I had known the pastor of the church in Alvin, and the church in Corpus was struggling. I soon realized I probably would never be a very good minister of education in a church atmosphere. I soon changed my major to that of business administration with a minor in religious education.

I have thought about this quite a bit over the years. Winnie was with me and encouraged me as we spent a little over two years for me to complete my studies and graduate. We spoke of it later as we came to Port Neches, me to work at Jefferson Chemical and she to continue her teaching career. I probably never would have returned to college for a business degree, but the urge to go back for a religious education degree made it happen. It worked out fine in the long run because I found a career in business but also used the religious education training in several church-oriented endeavors.

That was an interesting two years in Corpus Christi. One blessing was that we got to live near Pop, Mom, and the rest of Winnie's family. During one summer Winnie and I helped open another store in Tomball, and I did vacation relief for some of the stores to earn a little extra money, but mainly we depended on Winnie's earnings to exist.

Another thing happened that blessed our lives and continued to bless us. In October 1959 we welcomed a little palm-sized baby boy into our family. He did grow out of that!

33 Maggie and Me

I have referred to your mother many times in this writing. She contributed to both of our lives in uncountable ways. We were together, along with Tammie, when the emergency room person informed us she had left us. We were shocked because just hours before, we had been with her and had such promise that everything was going to be all right. Our friends and family joined us as we tried to mourn the passing of one so intricately woven into our lives. Sometime later, I wrote to try to express a little of the ongoing place she continues to share with us.

Her name was not Maggie. My Maggie was named Winnie Irene (Harris) Brown. Our childhoods were experienced many miles apart, but after 51-plus years together the tales and stories had been told and retold to meld our lives together so that they seemed almost common. Maggie could relate most of them better than me. After 31 years in the classroom and more than 20 in the study of Texas history, her storytelling was well-honed. This reached beyond the middle school classroom into her ability as Sunday school and Bible teacher.

A little red songbook was used by Texas school systems in the 30s and 40s as part of the music programs. *America Sings* provided schoolchildren of that era with such tunes as "When the Moon Comes Over the Mountain," "I'm Always Chasing Rainbows," "Little Brown Jug," "Londonderry Air," "Juanita," and "Grandfather's Clock." The little red book was a collection of patriotic songs, hymns, and folk tunes. Some of these were still being heard over our home radios, performed by our favorite singers of the time.

One tune that was probably bypassed was "When You and I Were Young, Maggie," written by George W. Johnson. There really wasn't much interest by the children of those days of singing about a long-ago love. As the years passed and the long-ago and lasting love became real, the words took on new meaning:

I wandered today to the hill, Maggie, to watch the scene below,

The creek and the old rusty mill, Maggie, where we sat in the long, long ago.
The green grove is gone from the hill, Maggie, where first the daisies sprung;
The old rusty mill is still, Maggie, since you and I were young.

They say we are feeble with age, Maggie, my steps less sprightly than then;
My face is a well-written page, Maggie, but time alone was the pen.
They say we are aged and gray, Maggie, as spray by the white breakers flung,
But to me you're as you were, Maggie, when you and I were young.

And now we are aged and gray, Maggie, the trials of life nearly done,
Let us sing of the days that are gone, Maggie, when you and I were young.

 I cannot visit a hill today to help recall all our experiences together. It is rather a flat place bordering the Neches River. At times large ocean-going vessels glide almost silently by. They are inbound and outbound mostly from places we only dreamed about or read about or perhaps the news on radio or television described. The river flows down to where the chemical plants and refineries do their work around the clock. The huge pecan trees of the area still try to live on, defying age and the ravages of the storms' winds.

 We did experience aging far beyond our expectations. A lot of our friends have gone. It was not a feeble aging that tested our physical as much as the body hurts of back and knees. We stayed our aging as much as possible by refusing to be defined by the hurts of the body we could hide. My Maggie's trials have ended so quickly. Her song of life lingers on and continues to touch those she loved so much.

 I'll remember some of our shared life and recall those stories and tales Maggie learned in my retelling.

34 The Hero

Heroes come in different forms, and we had one in our family. Jerry, my brother Neil's wife, can attest to that.

I was reminded of this hero a couple days ago when I read on Facebook a message that Peanut had died. Peanut, as you will remember, was a dog that greeted everyone who visited Neil and Jerry's home for many years. He was a Dachshund/terrier mix that enjoyed playing ball, and he became a tawny brown streak as he ran to retrieve the ball. He also had a wild side when pursuing a cat.

Peanut became a "hero" back in 2006.

Jerry had come into the house not feeling very well and bypassed Neil as he watched TV. She described herself as being dizzy and sick to her stomach. She did not realize and recognize the seriousness of her illness.

Jerry reached the bathroom before the stroke fully exerted itself and caused her to fall. She called as loudly as she could, but Neil, with the volume turned up, could not hear her.

There was another set of ears in the house that was alerted; Peanut streaked back to check out the situation. Jerry instructed Peanut to go get Neil.

Peanut followed Jerry's instruction and proceeded into the living room where Neil watched TV. Peanut wanted to talk, I'm sure, and began a whine that was almost human. Neil responded and followed him into the bedroom to find Jerry laying on the floor. He called 911.

Jerry had a lengthy stay in the hospital and rehab, regaining her basic skills, including learning to walk.

We all have agreed with Neil's assessment that Peanut saved Jerry's life. Jerry and Neil and their three sons—Ray, David, and Jeff—joined by all the family members and friends, will remember that special hero, Peanut. Here it is nine years later, and he has provided companionship and shared his nap in the recliner. After all, as a hero he got or did pretty much anything he wanted. RIP.

35 My Second Best Story

Although I perceive that most people think me to be humorless, I really enjoy a good story. Again, I am going to try to tell one I thought up myself and think is quite humorous.

When I take my auto to have the oil changed, I am reminded how oil once was changed. Now with the new super-lubricants, we go 5,000 to 10,000 miles between oil changes. Not many years ago, we were advised to have this done every 1,000 miles. Some of us chose another way; we went by the store that sold quarts of oil and purchased the number required so we could do the job ourselves.

The first requirement was to have a place for the oil change to be made. If you were fortunate enough to have a concrete driveway, that was a big plus. Some people, not so lucky, had oyster shell or just wheel ruts to park in for the change.

In my mind I pictured this as happening on a Saturday morning. I had made the proper purchases and parked the car as required. I lay on my back and scooted under the car and placed a vessel to catch the oil as it ran from the oil pan. I then used a wrench to loosen and unscrew the oil drain plug. The oil came pouring out as planned. After this is done, one needs to allow time for the oil to completely drain. I scooted out from under the car and went into the house for a sip of coffee.

As I was doing all this, Winnie was having a busy Saturday morning. She had been around the yard and house tending potted plants and may have cut a rose or two. As she came around the house, she viewed the car in the driveway with a body, from the waist down, and two legs extended from beneath the car. Winnie could be somewhat playful at times, and she saw a perfect opportunity. She quietly crept over to where the body could be viewed from the belt line down, and she could not resist. Quickly, she grabbed the zipper on the trousers and pulled it down.

I can attest that she really moved fast after accomplishing the feat. It was with a great deal of surprise to both of us—and especially to her—as she met me coming out of the house.

It was a much bigger surprise as we cast our eyes toward the car. There, sitting quite upright with a confused look and a streak of oil down his face, sat our neighbor. He had come over to lend a hand and was proceeding to replace the oil drain plug. There he sat with an imprint of the oil plug just about the center of his forehead.

I think it is marvelous that God has given us a mind that can take a little of the truth of everyday life and make it into a humorous tale. I count this as my second best story.

36 Brother-in-law Duncan

I was blessed with having the best brothers-in-law—Duncan and Orval—husbands of my sister Edith, along with super sisters-in-law—Maxine, Robbie's wife, and Jerry, Neil's wife. All have been a joy to the Brown family. I am just going to write about one, Duncan Taliaferro, at this time.

Duncan had come from meager circumstances and was always looking for a way to get ahead. During World War II metal was converted to the manufacture of war needs. This was before plastic became a replacement for metal. One of the items that had to change was the batons girls twirled with the hope of being featured in front of a band at football halftime and at other times when the band performed.

Duncan had an idea to accomplish the replacement of the metal tube that made the baton. He went to the lumber yard and purchased either 5/8 or half-inch dowels. He then visited the toy store and purchased rubber balls and crutch tips to complete the replacement baton. I believe he had some success with this, but it ended quickly when the war ended.

All good things come to an end, it seems. As the war ended and the metal batons began to appear, his wooden ones lost their appeal. Unfortunately, Duncan ended up with quite a supply of wooden dowels.

Some time passed before Duncan's enterprising mind found a way to rid himself of the dowels. When Duncan became a manager of a 5 and 10 store, one of the items the store sold was goldfish. The store had a fairly large glass container with a pump to circulate the air and a sandy, gravel bottom with various undersea-like figures displayed. At about this same time there was a fad beginning that made another fish pet rather popular. It was a little fish called a guppy.

I don't know the details, but Duncan became aware of a person who had a large fish pond or aquarium that was well supplied with guppies. Somehow Duncan made a deal with the person to trade his dowels for a lot of the little fish.

Now Duncan had to net the guppies and bring them to the store he operated and display them with the goldfish or instead of. I believe his sales must have been good because before long, I believe the other four stores in the chain were selling guppies.

Duncan passed away in 1961, but he left us with the joy he shared for living and an example of an entrepreneurial spirit like no other.

37 Hitch-hiking to Paris

At times old movies trigger memories. The 1946 movie *The Postman Always Rings Twice* triggers a memory for me today.

The story begins with a wanderer enjoying a ride from a kind driver. The wanderer had been taking advantage of what we call hitchhiking, standing beside the road with your thumb out, seeking a friendly driver to give you a lift. This was a quite acceptable means of travel for boys in their late teens and uniformed service personnel back in the 30s, 40s, and 50s. I used it to a great extent while in the Air Force because a person in uniform could, at times, make better time (and for less cost) than by bus or train. What I'm going to describe to you is about two kids getting a great idea with little planning.

I have written about three kids beginning first grade together; this somewhat follows up on that theme. Weldon (Roy) had come from California to visit relatives in the Malakoff area. Our friend, Roger Wayne, lived in Paris, Texas. I don't know how the idea came about, but Weldon and I determined that we would hitchhike to visit Roger.

I believe this may have been the first fairly long journey either of us had attempted traveling by the thumb method. I don't remember us having a map or not, but I suppose we may have consulted one in order to know the roads to travel. We must have been rather successful in our hitchhiking because we arrived on the Evans' doorstep late that afternoon. Mrs. Opal greeted us and, much to our amazement, advised us that Roger had gone by bus to visit his grandmother in Malakoff.

As I recall, Mrs. Opal treated us to a drink and something to eat. We were determined to go back as quickly as possible, and I believe she drove us to a good place on a road out of Paris. We must have been rather fortunate for the next part of the journey—Paris to Sulfur Springs—because that was where the next big decision had to be made.

On the outskirts of Sulfur Springs is a fork in the road. Either road will get you to Quitman, the next fairly large town. One route is a little longer. We tried both sides of the fork with little luck. There was one exception. On one fork we had several persons stop and offer us a ride, but they were all going to a place called Yantis.

Something in our minds told us to turn down the rides to Yantis. I think it was around 10:00 PM when, after a little discussion, we made the decision to take the next ride even if it was to Yantis. Logically, if there were that many persons going to Yantis, there has be someone going from there toward our way. The offer came quickly, and we were on our way.

Yantis is a place where a country road crosses the more traveled road that we traveled. Our ride stopped to let us out because they were turning. It was the intersection of the two roads. We emerged from the car, and as it drove away, we were in the darkness of night; I don't recall there being any visible light.

As all good hitchhikers do, we patiently waited for a while with no results. Eventually, we began to walk. Walking along the road we traveled at least moved us toward the next town. When and if a car came by to offer us a ride, we could accept.

Remember, we had been hitchhiking all day and by this time were approaching, if not past, midnight. A little rest or nap would be welcome. As I remember, it was a cornfield that beckoned us to rest a bit and perhaps nap. Even though it was a moonlit night and we were tired, nothing kept us from hearing the night sounds of the cornfield. It may have been the rustling of the cornstalks and leaves or the night critters that prowled the field. The rest period did not last long, and with a little fear and trembling our walking journey continued.

I believe it is about 10 or 12 miles from Yantis to Quitman, and we had walked a good part of that before a kindly gentleman gave us a ride. We arrived in Quitman around sunrise.

Don't remember too much about the trip on to Malakoff after this. Something about this story brings home to me that this thing called "friendship" is a part of our lives that is meaningful. I hope everyone has a friend or two who has been a part of his or her life.

One word of advice: "Call before going!"

38 Thoughts on Love

Varied thoughts come to me sometimes when I take my daily walk. Such a thing happened today as I made my journey around the block.

There is a verse in the Bible that means a lot to most Christians: "For now there are faith, hope, and love. But of the three, the greatest is love" (1 Cor 13:13 CEV).* As I walked, this verse and the word once used in the verse, *charity*, came to mind. Most later translations of this verse use the word *love*.

I have thought about this before, so it is not a new thought process for me. I really prefer the word *charity* in this verse. I suppose some of this thinking on my part is because the word *love* has been cheapened and overly used in our cultural language. *Charity* seems to have more meaning.

To have charity one must not only speak of it, but there must be an action that follows. I can say, "I love my neighbor," but if there is not some other action toward him expressing my caring for him, it is somewhat like Paul wrote: "Sounding brass, or a tingling cymbal."

Jesus, it seems to me, demonstrated his love by meeting the needs of those he encountered. His "charity" included the teaching of his apostles, restoring the sight to the blind, healing the sick, exhorting the unbelievers to understand, and ultimately giving his life for even me.

Real love can be experienced in many ways. Just because I do not say or repeat it often doesn't mean it cannot be shown. I believe this is why charity has a more meaningful understanding for me. If one loves another, he will respond by showing the person with his actions of meeting needs and wants.

There is a song that includes the words "I love you for sentimental reasons." That is a beautiful expression, but without a meaningful expression continuing beyond the words, it becomes a passing moment's expression.

I hope to some degree I have met the test of being charitable to all I have been called to love.

39 Smokey Airplane

I do not remember being scared too many times in my life, but there have been occasions when after the fact I was a little beyond concerned. So it was with the following incident.

I went to the flight line to board a B-25 in order to get the required flying hours so I would be paid flight pay for the month. Several of the radar mechanics were on flight status in order to ascertain and possibly repair in-flight radar problems that were not experienced when ground checks were made of the radar systems.

We had the normal taxi to our place in line for takeoff. After the taxi and warmup check the plane made the run for takeoff and began the climb toward flight altitude departure point for Ellington Field. Wheels up and cool feelings were normal experiences of takeoff.

It was very soon after takeoff that the interphone headset came on with an alert from either a student or instructor in the rear compartment of the plane: "Smoke coming into the plane from the wing root!" This triggered a quick response from everyone who had a headset on—an automatic check of the parachute harness and straps.

I was in the radio compartment and entryway behind the pilot and co-pilot. The pilot motioned to me and instructed me to cut off the electrical system for the plane. The plane's engine would operate on a magneto system.

Another person had boarded the plane for the flight today and had quickly crawled through the entryway to the nose section of the plane (bombardier's position in combat). The pilot motioned to me again and asked that I notify the fellow up front to return to the radio compartment. When I cut off the electric system, it meant the intercom system ceased to operate also. That entryway was somewhat like a tunnel running under the pilot's elevated position. To transverse the tunnel required that I remove my parachute. I quickly crawled far enough into the tunnel to gain the man's attention and motion for him to come out. He quickly followed.

As this was occurring, the pilot was turning to circle the plane back into a position so we could enter the upwind landing pattern. With no interplane communication, the three persons in the back were unaware of what was happening. The pilot had another idea.

The pilot motioned to me again. He wanted to test the emergency alarm system, and he did not want those in back to bail out. I was to crawl through another small tunnel over the bomb bay and tell them it was just a test. This also required that I shed my parachute and crawl as far as possible by the radar and electric equipment that occupied most of the space over the bomb bay. The check was made, and I returned to the radio compartment.

I once again strapped on my parachute. I have thought about this afterward and wonder if the worst had developed and leaving the plane had been ordered, would we have been high enough for the use of a parachute? After strapping myself to the chute, the other person and I opened the flooring door of our compartment. We could view the ladder steps used to enter and leave the front compartments and were ready to depart after landing and coming to a stop.

As soon as the plane stopped, we dropped the ladder for quick exit, and as soon as the propellers stopped turning, the two of us deplaned. As I remember, I thought we were deplaning rather quickly, but those three guys who were in the back already had their cigarettes lit by the time I got from under the plane. Guess they may have run the last 50 yards or so!

I began this writing with a comment about fear or being scared. I believe, from my experience, when an emergency situation comes to us, there is little time or place for fear. In this case we came to a safe landing. The crew chief, after examining one of the engines, related that the starter on that engine had failed to disengage, which caused it to overheat and burn the lubricants and insulation around it.

As I wrote this, another short remembrance came to me.

I do not remember if this happened before or after the story I just completed. It was a rainy evening, almost dark. Those in the barracks and on the base heard a jet plane make a pass overhead and diminish out of hearing. A short time later, the jet returned. As it was almost directly overhead, there was a tremendous explosion. The entire crew perished, as I remember. The plane more than likely was on some kind of training mission. I believe it was a B-45 out of Shreveport, Louisiana. Jets were relatively new to the Air Force, and I believe this was a plane that was to replace one of the WWII propeller-driven planes.

Fate or luck when emergencies are upon us? If you have one, you will have some remembrance.

Harold Brown Writes*

COUNTERACTION

The Songs of a Nation

No matter what the circumstances a man may be encountering in this life of pain and pleasure, he can usually thrust forth himself and relieve his tensions by breaking forth into song. The song may be a lament to his providential displeasure. In like manner the song may be a tale of enchanted joy. Forlorn is the man who cannot raise his soul in some semblance of song.

America has always been a land filled with the music of its people. The soul of the nation has almost burst with pride as the hills, valleys, and plains vibrated to the strains of its music. "Yankee Doodle," The Star Spangled Banner," "Camptown Races," "Mine Eyes Have Seen the Glory," "Swing Low, Sweet Chariot," "St. Louis Blues," "I've Been Working on the Railroad"—these are just a few of the songs of America. These are not only the songs of America; here is the soul of America.

There is one song that could not go unmentioned in thinking of the music of America. The strains of music are borrowed from the motherland of England, but the words could only rightfully belong to America: "My country, 'tis of thee, sweet land of liberty, of thee I sing." This is a song relating the entailment of all with which we can justly be proud.

The chorus of the stout-hearted people of our land is not as robust and hail as it has been in past times. It is not the roar of twentieth-century rockets or the clashing and clanging of modern-day industrial activity that will drown out the songs of the nation. The chorus will only be quieted when the soul of the nation becomes forlorn because it has lost all hope.

The last verse of "America" may hold the clue in its prayer-like phrasing: "Long may our land be bright with freedom's holy light; protect us by thy might, great God our king."

40 Ollie and Golf

One of the persons I worked with and continue a relationship with is Ollie. I believe you and I have gone on a couple duck- or goose-hunting trips with him.

Ollie is somewhat of a perfectionist. When he becomes interested in something, he will study and explore the workings and ramifications of the subject. For example, when he became interested in hunting larger game like elk and deer, it required some understanding and knowledge of a fairly large caliber of rifle. He not only practiced by shooting targets but also studied the various calibers, trajectories, and characteristics of the shells and bullets that could be used.

So it was when, for a time, he became interested in the game of golf. The selection of proper clubs and balls was important. He then practiced and studied the use of the various clubs: drivers, irons, putters, etc., under various circumstances. He became quite good at proper selection of clubs, and since he physically strong, he did very well on the golf course.

I had acquired some used golf clubs and had puttered around on the nine-hole golf course in Groves. There came a day when Ollie and I decided to put our golf skills together. There was an old golf course on Pleasure Island across the ship channel from the city of Port Arthur, and this is where we chose to display our golfing know-how with a round of golf.

I do not remember if this incident happened on the ninth or eighteenth hole of the course. As I remember, both holes had tee boxes, fairways, and greens that led back toward the clubhouse. Whichever hole, it was positioned so that the fairway ran parallel to the ship channel. This meant the tee box was also adjacent to the ship channel.

It was Ollie's time to make his drive off the tee box so that the ball would fly down the fairway parallel to the channel. He most carefully teed up the ball and made a couple practice swings to ensure the alignment was perfect for the fairway.

Now, I have seen Ollie study everything to gain as much expertise as possible. I am sure he took all of his knowledge into account as he approached the ball.

Ollie put all his power into that swing and aim as the club head contacted the ball. His follow-through was completed, and he reached the peak of his swing. Then the unimaginable happened! The power of the swing continued to such an extent that the driver separated from his hand and began its flight out toward the ship channel. I know it didn't go that far, but it looked as if it traveled to the middle of the channel.

Ollie was one frustrated and surprised person as his gaze followed that club to its final resting place. We can recall such an incident now with some degree of glee and mirth, but as we continued toward the green that day, we were less elated.

41 Pop and the Fresno

I suspect that every once in a while, your memory brings to mind something about Pop Harris. His name was Gilbert, but everyone knew him as Bill. There are many tales that can be told about him.

In the 1930s Pop and Mom had already started their family, with Winnie being the first and Helen arriving sometime later. Kay came along a lot later. Life was not easy for them. Pop had farmed and perhaps tried to have a cow or two. Both Mom and Pop came from rather large families, so they had experienced the struggles of day-to-day life. They knew about sharing and making do with what was present in life.

During the 1930s in Bee County, a new enterprise had arisen: drilling for oil and finding natural gas. It gave employment to some, but to Pop it presented an idea and a challenge. He observed that when a well was drilled, there had to be amenities provided. There had to be "slush pits"—dammed-up areas that could receive and hold excess liquids from the well. These had to be constructed for each well by scooping out dirt from the interior of a circle or semi-square and piling the dirt around the circumference to form a dam.

I believe Pop already had part of the requirements for providing a service for the constructing of these slush pits. He had four mules: Jake, Bell, Minnie, and Emma (note: After he left the slush pit construction business and the mules needed to be sold, he was careful in the sale to assure the mules would be cared for properly. He would visit them and only needed to whistle to call them to the fence).

The other need was for a piece of equipment called a Fresno. The Fresno had been invented in the 1800s for use in moving certain kinds of dirt for dams or channels. Some had been used for the construction of the Panama Canal.

The Fresno was a scraper that could be pulled by mules or horses. As the Fresno was pulled along the ground, an operator could set the blade in a manner that it would scrape into the ground, and its curved back allowed the soil to be accumulated for movement. When the container was full, the operator moved the handle so the soil was retained, and it would be dragged to the place where it would be dumped to form part of a retaining dam or revetment.

Pop had the mules and, with a partner, arranged for a couple Fresnos. They were in the business of constructing slush pits. They developed a good business, and eventually Pop purchased the partner's share from his partner's widow after his death. I believe this provided a good income for Pop and his family, but he was also able to provide employment for extended family members.

Pop built up quite a reputation as a businessman and worker. This served him well in later years as he was elected to positions of county commissioner and Bee County treasurer.

42 The Mexican Mission

I left the Air Force in 1952 after serving four years. I had originally enlisted for three years, but the United States became involved in an undeclared war with North Korea during my enlistment, so I had an extra year added. I took a short time after the discharge and visited Malakoff.

Prior to leaving the Air Force, I had been offered a job with the McLemore Variety Store chain. Sister Edith and brother-in-law Duncan had been involved with the stores and were both managing stores in Port Neches and Groves. To begin with, my involvement with the stores was to be a training period of about three years under the GI Bill (the Government was to pay part of my salary during this training time).

After beginning my training in Alvin, I quickly moved my church membership to the First Baptist Church of Alvin. During my Air Force time I had not been active in a church. It was ironical; I found that the church I was affiliating with had been led into a rather huge debt situation by a minister who had previously been in Malakoff. One of the blessings of this church to me was the new pastor. The church, although struggling under the minister's leadership, was working its way out of the problems facing it. This minister blessed Winnie and me again as our pastor when we were in Corpus Christi.

After aligning with the church, I discovered it had a mission project among the Mexican citizens of Alvin. I became acquainted with the mission pastor and some of the FBC members who were involved in that ministry.

The mission was meeting in a house the church had acquired. I believe this was among the first ministries of this type sponsored by a Texas Baptist church that was directed to the Mexican people in a local community.

It was evident that the mission effort needed all the help it could muster. One of the outstanding needs was a larger and better place for worship and training. I, along with the pastor and others from FBC, began encouraging more monetary support.

Several of those at the mission also began to think in terms of what kind of structure could be built with the least amount of money. We found there was a company in the Houston area that made an oversized concrete brick. We came up with a floor plan and got together a cost figure for walls and slab.

By having some figures and a plan to present to the FBC pastor and finally to the church for approval, progress was made. It happened the church had a bond program that incurred the debt they were dealing with. Either all the bonds had not been sold or someone had presented back to the church bonds that had been purchased. There were bonds available. The church voted to go forward with the building of a mission building. When the bonds were sold, as I remember, it was about $2,000 or $3,000.

This was my first excursion into ministry like this. It was successful, and after a time and with use of the funds and some laymen craftsmen, the mission worship center became a reality and a very good contribution to the Mexican community of Alvin.

I believe this church was ahead of most Baptist churches in reaching out on a local level to the Latino population. Most persons at that time considered that population to be the haven of the Catholic denomination.

43 Grocery Store Changes

I am continually amazed as I walk the aisles of my favorite grocery store at the tremendous numbers and various products for the customer to choose from.

The little Gulf Market where I worked during my high school years did not offer such choice. Very few items offered more than one or two choices, and then probably in one size. I believe this was true in most grocery stores of the day.

There was another big difference in how some of the items were offered and how they were prepared for sale. I know you'll remember I have written about this, but think about how different it is today. The navy beans, pinto beans, and sugar, for instance, arrived in as much as 100-pound sacks. Some items had large storage drawers assigned to them, and after a bag was dumped into the drawer, the beans, sugar, etc., had to be bagged into sellable sizes. Brown paper bags were used for beans and sugar. I don't remember the exact sizes for each item, but lima beans might have been bagged in 1- or 2-pound bags where pinto beans may have been 2- and 5-pound bags. As I recall, the sugar was bagged in two sizes: 5 pounds and 10 pounds. The sugar was rationed, and I believe this set the normal amounts allotted to families. The top of the bags, after filling, were neatly folded and taped shut, then stacked in the proper storage area assigned.

Other items that came to the store in bulk were cookies. I believe these were in boxes of 25 pounds. There was a cookie that was similar to the Oreo of today, and I think it came in chocolate and vanilla sides with a white filling. These were bagged in cellophane bags by the dozen, I believe.

My favorite cookie to sack was the Fig Newton. They would slide into the cellophane bag easily, and they made a nice, inviting package to the customer. They were probably my favorite because they were my favorite cookie. Something happened, though, that changed my preference for cookies. Just about every box of cookies had some that would be broken or damaged. Of course, they had to be taken care of by consuming the tasty treats. That's what happened to me and the Fig Newton. After disposing of something just shy of a carload of Fig Newtons, over time I lost my taste for them. Only recently have I regained an enjoyment for them.

Another interesting item that arrived occasionally was a large wire-bound crate containing side meat (salt pork). Everyone, it seemed, cooked their vegetables and dried beans with salt pork. This was sold by the customer telling the clerk how much they wanted. The clerk would estimate how much was a pound or whatever was needed. Then it was weighed for proper weight charges. Occasionally, people would slice the salt pork and fry it; Mama, as I remember, did this a few times. The salt would be scraped away prior to frying. Today you are lucky to find a small piece of salt pork at the grocery store, and it is higher in cost than bacon, for which it had been substituted in days past. Between the salt and fat that made up most of salt pork, it is now frowned upon as being unhealthy.

Another unusual sight by today's standards was Gulf Market's way of displaying our bananas. The banana man came through and delivered the bananas still on the stalk. The stalk was then hung in a corner of the store out of the foot traffic. When the customer wanted bananas, either the clerk or customer would take a knife and cut off the appropriate number of bananas.

Gulf Market did not do this, but a larger grocery store downtown purchased eggs. The people in the surrounding area would collect the eggs and, especially on Saturday, bring them to town and sell them. The grocery store would purchase the eggs, and the clerks would put the eggs in a crate; I believe each crate would hold 30 dozen. When full, the crate was closed and placed in a cooler to await the arrival of the person who would purchase the eggs and truck them away.

Since I have gone away from the Gulf Market store, I must tell you about the deal Grandmamma made with another grocery store several years before I worked at Gulf Market. She made a deal with the grocery store downtown to buy some of our extras from the garden: green onions, carrots, radishes, and maybe turnip greens. These could be bundled into small batches for easy sale.

One time, Grandmamma bundled up some of these items and sent me to the store to trade for a list of groceries. It happened that on that weekend, there was a sale of cabbage. I believe it was 1 cent per pound. My instructions were as follows: If there is any left after you fill the purchase on the list, get some cabbage. As I remember, there remained some 10 or 12 cents, so I got one huge cabbage head. I believe we had cabbage dishes for quite a few days after that.

Don't ever wish for the "good old days" when Admiration coffee was 33 cents a pound and it didn't come in a can. Now you can choose anywhere from the store brand to Starbucks, but I will tell you it will cost a little more than 33 cents a pound.

44 A Little Lung Problem

You will probably remember part of this writing, but you were young and will only remember some that involved you.

It was to be an exciting and eventful time on the Memorial Day weekend of 1961. Mom and Pop had come from Corpus Christi, and on Sunday arrangements had been made to meet Azalee and Ted (Mom's sister and husband) somewhere in Louisiana; they lived in Baton Rouge.

I don't recall exactly what happened. I either coughed very hard (I did smoke) or swallowed something that made me cough. Whatever it was left me with a most terrible cough and a little tightness in my chest.

The day had been planned, and I'm sure I grabbed a handful of cough drops. Off we went to the meeting and enjoyment of lunch together with Azalee and Ted. The cough did not get better through the day and night.

Sometime Monday, I decided I had better go see Dr. Byrd to determine the cause of such a terrific and lasting cough. He made his examination and explained to me that I had a muscle spasm in my chest and gave me a prescription for a muscle relaxant.

I believe I may have waited two days to return to Dr. Byrd and tell him the relaxants were not working very well. I still had the terrific cough and tightness of the chest. The doctor said that there needed to be an x-ray of my chest to see what might be occurring.

The x-ray was done, and I found a seat close to the room where developing was done. Seems like even today I can visualize the nurse coming out of that developing room and scurrying past with no comment or recognition. She just blew by me and up the hallway.

Momentarily, Dr. Byrd and the nurse came hurrying down the hall and made their way to the dark room. Shortly after, Dr. Byrd called me to come and see the x-ray and pointed out that the right side of my chest cavity was almost vacant and then pointed out where the lung rested against the middle wall of my body (this was why I had such a cough, as the lung irritated itself). I have always described the lung as being about the size of a 5-cent balloon, but nobody knows what that is. Look at your thumb, and take that as a size and shape of the visible lung.

Of course, that required a trip to the local hospital in the edge of Port Arthur for a procedure. Into the operating room I went, and the doctor met me with a rather large syringe with needle attached. Instead of injecting a fluid into me, the procedure was reversed. The needle was inserted through my rib cage and used to draw out the air in the cavity. Whatever happened that Sunday morning had caused a bleb (a lung imperfection) to pop and force all the air in the lung into the chest cavity. Slowly, the air was withdrawn until the lung had expanded to almost touch the needle and the chest wall. Everything went fine, and I was sent home for a time to allow the lung and chest to absorb the remaining air and give the lung time to heal the pop-out.

It was during this time I had an event happen that was at least embarrassing if not more. I had not been able to do the normal activities around the house if it required exertion or straining. One of those things was mowing the lawn. It had been quietly growing. After some time, I was feeling great, and I decided that I could take it very easy and not push or pull too much, I could mow the yard. During the mowing a strange auto pulled up to the side of the street in front of the house. I could have crawled under that lawnmower! It was the personnel manager from the plant, Mr. Parker. This was the same person who had called me back after the interview to tell me he had a job opening after all. I survived that and returned to work as soon as the doctor released me.

Fast-forward a few days. I always took my lunch to work and normally ate it at my desk. My workplace was down in the plant in the shipping and receiving area. Whatever my sandwich or soft drink was for the day, some of it tried to go down the wrong way. What do you do when that happens? You cough.

There was another cough, and with it a return of a terrific cough and tightness in the chest. It was back to the doctor.

After an examination by Dr. Byrd, I was told that what had been done before was not a treatment that could be done again. The doctor said because of how long the lung had been in some stage of collapse that the lining of the chest cavity and outside of the lung could be drying and could cause long-term damage. He arranged for me to go see a thoracic surgeon.

Winnie and I motored to Houston for proper tests and examinations. Surgery was the option, and a date was set. We had to return home, and arrangements were made for us to meet Mom and Pop somewhere down Highway 59 on Sunday so you, Paul, could go and stay with them for a while.

Monday came, and the surgery was performed at St. Joseph Hospital in Houston. The surgeon had a special wing and floor of the hospital to care for his patients. One reason for his special place was that he was somewhat ahead of his time. No laying around in bed after surgery. The best I remember, I had to sit up on the side of the bed that night and was consistently reminded to cough. Next morning, I believe, they made me get out of bed so the bed clothes could be changed. The nurses and nuns had the doctor's instructions to get the patient up and on the move. His reasoning, as he explained it to me, was you invited pneumonia by laying around and not exercising and coughing the liquid up from the lungs. So that is what the nurses and sisters required, and I got up and walked as soon as possible.

The operation consisted of the removing of one rib so the surgeon could find the bleb in the lung so it could be closed. A tube was inserted to draw off the accumulation of liquid in the chest cavity after closure. The lung then was allowed to inflate. Part of the surgery was for the removal of the pleura (chest lining). Once the lung was inflated, it would now adhere to the chest wall.

I believe either on Wednesday or Thursday, 9 or 10 days after the surgery, I was discharged from the hospital and Winnie drove us to Corpus Christi. On that Saturday I had to be back in Houston to see the doctor for a checkup.

"When can I return to work?" I asked.

"You are okay to work!"

Then he gave me some good advice: "If it hurts, don't do it."

I returned to work on Monday, exactly two weeks after the surgical operation. I believe the doctor was correct: you just can't lay around after an operation. It was with a great deal of apprehension that the plant nurses cleared me to go back to my job that Monday morning. I am pretty sure a telephone call was made to the surgeon for confirmation that morning.

There was a reason I needed to return to work as soon as possible. I had not been with Jefferson Chemical long enough to have any sick time off. If I didn't work, I didn't get paid.

I learned a couple things from this episode in my life that have given me better understanding. One is that people are good and compassionate. Two or three times during the time I dealt with this lung problem, a person would arrive at my home and present me with cash. Remember, I had not been working at Jefferson Chemical very long and was not widely acquainted around the plant. Word had been passed around about my not having any benefits, and money was collected. I was attempting to get back on my feet financially from my late return to college when this occurred. I am eternally grateful to those unknowns who gave me a helping hand.

Another thing I learned has contributed to a lot of thought in my relationship to God. The surgeon, in his explanation prior to surgery, advised about the removal of a rib. He also explained that the covering of the rib would be retained and kept in place. He indicated that within a short time, my body would replace that rib; it would grow back. As I recall, this is the only bone in the body that will replace itself. X-rays today confirm that I have a rib there, although it is not quite as pretty and straight like the others.

Now consider this. When the Bible tells us about God removing Adam's rib to make him a helpmate, did God consider in his choice for material for Eve that "after I do this, old Adam will just regrow his rib"? That should start you to thinking!

45 High School Football

I am writing this during fall, when all around the land, a lot of conversation is about football. You know how much this is a part of Port Neches, where you grew up and became an "Indian."

Football was an important sport at Malakoff High School and the community during the 1930s and 1940s, but during the first three years of my time there, we did not have a football team. I suppose there were several reasons: The coal mines had closed, and the student population had decreased. The war had caused other families to move away and also decreased the number of students. Lastly, and probably most importantly, was that the young men who would be coaches had been drafted.

When I was beginning my senior year, there was a stirring among the male students to have a football team. The principal of the high school was available to be the coach. We were going to have a football team!

I had worked at Gulf Market the year before, and I chose to resign that position or work only part time so I could come out for the football team. At 130 pounds I was not an imposing figure in a football uniform. At the drugstore I got an over-the-counter product that was supposed to put weight on my skinny body. I also drank a lot of milkshakes and malted milkshakes to help put on weight.

Restarting football from scratch like this had its problems. Uniforms were those from years gone by, and the leather pads and shoes were stiff and well worn. I know some, if not all of the linemen's shoes actually had wooden cleats. As I remember, the school did purchase a few pairs of shoes for those trying for the backfield.

As I remember, no one who presented themselves to play that fall in 1945 had ever played a down of high school football. I guess most of us had played sandlot or playground football, but "real" football is quite different.

The coach was trying to prepare us to play. We started late, so he was able to schedule only two games, and they were with the same school, Eustace. The training consisted of trying to train us to play both ways, offense and defense. As I remember, I was to learn the plays as an offensive backfield person; this was before the T, so it may have been called halfback. I also had to learn a little defense as a line-backing position. I believe we had about six weeks' preparation before the first game.

I believe it was the Wednesday before the first scheduled game on Friday that my football career came to a screeching halt. One of the exercises the coach had us do that day was what was termed a rolling block. This is where the blocker would run toward the person being blocked and throw his body into the legs under the other person. This exercise was done by lining up the team members into two lines: One line would be the blocker, and the other would be the receiver of the block. When it came my time to block, I looked across to see my friend Delroy, who was probably the biggest person on the field. I tried to block him. Then we lined up again, but we changed lines. I looked up to see the person who would roll into me with all his size—it was Delroy. I don't remember how many times these two things happened, but it was always Delroy.

I do remember the last block. I was to block him and tried as best I could to roll myself into him so he would be knocked off his feet. I think his feet did go somewhere, because when he came down, he sat on me. Something happened! My left side felt different. I don't know if I really knew at this point what the problem was, but I knew it was something that needed attention.

Since we only had the one coach, he could not leave all the others, so I had to make my way to the gym locker room to don my street clothes. As I finished dressing, Danny came into the room and asked if he could drive me to the doctor's office. Dr. Kilman examined me, and I believe he took an x-ray before he determined I had broken my collarbone on the left side.

The doctor and his nurse fitted me with what I call a T-brace. It extended down my back to about belt height and across my upper shoulders. This was metal. There were straps that were around my waist and also under my armpits. After being strapped up, I had to walk the short distance home. Made it back to school the next day.

Friday found a busload of Malakoff Tigers headed out to Eustace for the first ballgame. My seat was a seat with a view, looking out the back window of the bus. This was a long bus; I believe they called it a 40-footer. The seats were located with a row of the seat backs to each side of the bus and then a row down the middle where persons could sit with their backs together. This middle row offered me a place to sit because the seats stopped short of the door and I could sit with my back against nothing. Remember, I was wearing the T-brace, but I could hold steady by looping my good arm around the seat back.

Everything was going good, and the team could hardly wait to play their first game. Then the bus had a blowout! You can imagine how much a 40-foot bus can careen with the driver fighting to keep it on the road because the shoulder of the road is rather steep. I was holding on for dear life.

We made it to the game site, and the Tigers lost the game, but I believe a couple years later some of these boys put together a team that won district and I believe had one of the best records of any Tigers team.

This ended my football-playing experience. I still enjoy watching the game. Now, in addition to the high schools, we have college and pros to watch on television. I marvel at the precision and athletic abilities we see in the players today. The Tigers are still playing, and the community of Malakoff is still giving them great support. So I yell for the Tigers, the Indians, the Texans, the Cowboys, and the Aggies now.

46 Another of My Stories

I have written about the best two stories that I believe I originated with the help of a few real-life experiences. My story here is not original but does have the names of a couple real-life people. I believe I heard at some time the gist of the story, but the names of these two people just seemed too good not to use.

We did have an uncle and aunt with the names of George and Georgia. Aunt Georgia was my father's sister, and of course they were raised in the community of Cayuga, Anderson County, Texas. Uncle George was from a rather prominent family, also in Cayuga. That's not saying a lot, but I believe the family had some land holdings in the area, and this boded well for them when oil drilling came to the area.

Uncle George died during the 1940s, but Aunt Georgia lived for many years and at some point moved to the Waco area, where her son, Henry, and family lived. Henry taught school after college but eventually lived in the Waco area and I believe was in the insurance business. Anyway, that all is said to say I borrowed their names for this story because they sound appropriate.

Now, the story begins after the namesake Uncle George has recently passed to the great beyond. After a time of mourning, the other namesake, Aunt Georgia, had begun to think about her own demise. Now, these two had been among the most frugal persons in the community. In fact, Uncle George had been known as being "tight as Dick's hat band" (that's an old East Texas saying).

Aunt Georgia, as she planned to take care of all the arrangements for her own passing, acted in a prudent and frugal manner. She confided in a dear niece. The niece accompanied her and provided the transportation to the cemetery for those accommodations. A trip to the local funeral director and a choice for the proper casket were made. Then to the florist and finally a stop by the minister's office. Aunt Georgia had thought she had covered every item required to be "put away" proper. She had neglected one.

As the niece drove into Aunt Georgia's driveway, the niece asked if she had selected her dress or gown for the occasion. Aunt Georgia had not given thought to her burial clothes. They selected a date to shop for this item.

The niece arrived on the appointed day, and they decided to go to the county seat city to shop for that item. There were larger department stores and dress shops there. They had visited several stores before eventually they arrived at a store that was having a sale on some really beautiful and recently higher priced gowns and dresses. After much looking and feeling of material and designs, a full-length garment was chosen. The purchase was made for a very decent price. The niece and Aunt Georgia motored home, believing all needs had been met for Aunt Georgia's demise.

A couple days after the shopping trip, the niece heard a knock on her door and opened it to find Aunt Georgia with this fairly large package in her arms. She informed her niece she had bought some material that could be made into dresses for the niece's two young daughters.

As the package was unwrapped, the niece looked with a sense of awe. The material seemed to be exactly like the gown Aunt Georgia had purchased. Aunt Georgia then began to explain that the gown was just too full and long to be buried in and that she had cut it off a few inches below the waist line. The niece was somewhat speechless.

After a momentary pause the niece said to Aunt Georgia, "You shouldn't have done that. What are you going to do in heaven when you have to stand there in a cutoff gown? You will be embarrassed!"

Aunt Georgia waited until the niece had voiced her opposition and then with a little East Texas "tee-hee" said to the niece, "Honey, don't you worry about that because nobody will be looking at me. You see, I buried your Uncle George without his pants!"

So it's a borrowed story that probably only I would like.

47 The Halloween Carnival

In my freshman or sophomore year in high school, a young lady came to Malakoff High School as the music teacher and band director. I believe she came directly out of college because she was quite young, seemingly not much older than the seniors in the band. I believe I learned more music under her direction, which was a one-year stay, than any other I ever experienced. It was a one-year stay because of a particular activity she proposed and carried through with, but that is getting ahead of the story.

Sometime in late September or early October, she began to work with the band members and others (I am sure the high school principal and/or the superintendent had to bless it) to have a Halloween carnival in the gymnasium. As I remember, it was a fund-raising event to benefit the band for music and possibly instruments.

Everyone seemed to get into the planning and preparation for the occasion. I believe both Neil and I were part of these activities. Remember, the school did not have football, so any activity at this time of the year would have been welcome.

Something really bad happened! Our mother found out—along with a lot of other Baptist mothers, I'm sure—that this horribly bad band director was also proposing a dance to be held after the Halloween carnival was over. The two of us were informed that we would not be attending the Halloween carnival because there was going to be a dance.

I recall this again after all these years because that young lady was not the band director the next year. It is my belief that because she proposed that dance, there were complaints from persons like my mother to the school and her contract was not renewed. That is just my idea. I do not know how many attended the dance or, for that matter, the Halloween carnival. I do know one thing: If that is the reason she did not return, Malakoff High School was deprived of one of the best music teachers and band directors.

48 Churches

Church has always been an important part of my life. I have mentioned several churches in my writings but not presented a very good picture of its importance.

Of course, my church experience began early in my life in Malakoff. Some of my early remembrances can go back there. It was this church that nurtured me in the 1930s and until I departed for the Air Force in 1948. Various leaders and teachers imprinted my relationship with God: Father, Son, and Holy Spirit. I learned some of the rudiments of Christianity: worship, music, involvement, missions, and a little about church leadership.

My Air Force time was really outside the church's influence. I just never found a place or the time to be involved for this period of time. Of course, I did occasionally return to attend services at the First Baptist Church in Malakoff.

After leaving the Air Force I realigned myself with church by joining the First Baptist Church in Alvin. I have already related some of my experiences there, but the most important part of being there was the influence on the pastor and a woman who worked in the Training Union (youth group) program. I observed through the pastor leadership skills not present in most pastors of the era. The Training Union woman also utilized leadership and training skills not employed by many persons I had been acquainted with in the Training Unions at church.

As related in an earlier writing, I experienced the feeling that I could contribute some skills to influencing and carrying out plans that benefited groups of Christians trying to worship and spread the gospel.

After leaving Alvin I went to West Columbia and for a short time was a member of the First Baptist Church there. I did not stay in that church very long but joined with a group of persons in the Wild Peach community. Someone had given a parcel of land to a group trying to start a church in that community located between West Columbia and Brazoria. Before I arrived, they had acquired a tent and built some benches and were holding services with a lay pastor as preacher. I believe I did make some contribution to this endeavor. Because of some of my experience in the construction of a building in Alvin, within a short time the Wild Peach Baptist Church had a church building. Some of my first dates with Winnie were to this church.

Not long after Winnie and I married, I had an opportunity to open a variety store in La Porte. We joined the Bayshore Baptist Church soon after getting settled in La Porte. This church had a great influence on our lives. I began to feel like I should go into religious education, and Winnie and I began exploring an idea of going back to college. I had about a year and a half, so we were looking at two-plus years at best. I guess one thing that influenced us to a degree was the pastor felt he needed to go to Hawaii and start a ministry. He tried getting appointed as missionary by the Southern Baptist Mission Board, but I believe his wife had medical problems and he could not be appointed. He just packed up and went anyway. Some of that may have rubbed off on us.

In exploring our opportunities we visited Mom and Pop in Corpus Christi, and we drove around the University of Corpus Christi, a Texas Baptist institution. As I have related a very important part of the decision was what happened on this trip, guess God intervened. Winnie had a thought. She knew a principal in the Flour Bluff school system and decided to call to see if there might be a chance at a teaching job if we came to Corpus. She made the call and, at the insistence of the friend, went to a meeting with the superintendent of the district. When she came back, she had been offered a job. Mind you, she was not "properly dressed" and had no credentials to show the superintendent. I guess this made up our minds that I was to return to college. I still must think that the influence of the La Porte church had something to do with the thought process to go back to college.

After leaving La Porte and moving to Corpus Christi, I enrolled in the University of Corpus Christi and soon united with Calvary Baptist Church. This was primarily influenced by my having known the pastor while a member of the Alvin church. After a period of time, I worked as a part-time education director for the church. This also had a huge influence on our lives. I came to realize that I was not a "people person" and probably could never fit into the mold of what a full-time education director or minister would require. I did not have the charisma or personage for people that Pop, Winnie, and you were blessed with.

I changed my major to business administration with a minor in religious education. I believe that without the thought of pursuing a "church work" education at the college level, I never would have returned to continue my education. I owe it all to the patience and encouragement of Winnie. I believe we were blessed in future years. We came away from Corpus with you! You joined us in Corpus, and upon my graduation we came to Port Neches. It was not long after arriving that we found ourselves at Southside Baptist and I found myself in a role in which I never could have pictured myself.

At Southside I was invited to be the music director and served in that capacity a couple times. Of course, you can remember some of that time because you enjoyed a front-row seat for a great deal of the time. The time at Southside gave me the opportunity of overcoming, to some degree, the fear of appearing before people in a leadership role. This fear had been instigated by an experience in grade school (that's another story).

After a time Winnie and I sensed that our time at Southside needed to change, primarily because you did not have children of your age to associate with. We three, you had made a profession of faith to me, joined First Baptist of Port Neches.

A short time after we joined First Baptist, I became involved with the Woodcrest mission project sponsored by the church. Brother Sasser and several other persons from the church held teaching and preaching services in a converted apartment, Woodcrest, a low-rent housing development. I was able to use some of my religious education training I had learned at college and in other churches. The use of the music experienced at Southside was of vital importance in working with the people at Woodcrest. The Woodcrest development was condemned and to be torn down, so this led to a new location. This location did not work very well for the persons involved in the Woodcrest situation. The people had been scattered after leaving Woodcrest.

Although I did not attend a lot at First Baptist, I believe it worked to the advantage of Winnie and you. You especially got to be a part of a very active youth group, and I believe it allowed you to enjoy your church relationship.

After a time I received a call from Brother Sasser. He had taken on a responsibility of pastoring Woodcrest Baptist Church in Port Arthur. The church had experienced a downturn in membership and leadership and was struggling. He needed a music director to help with worship. Winnie and I went there to be a part of this endeavor to revitalize the church. Winnie helped in the organization of the office work, and I tried to provide leadership in a music program. The church began to make some progress, but an incident occurred that I believed to be unlawful, or otherwise morally wrong, on the part of an individual. Winnie and I withdrew and returned to Southside.

Brother Sasser remained at Woodcrest and shepherded it through a tremulous time. The church became somewhat healthy, and an economic blessing came to them that allowed a move of location and continued place of worship and teaching.

Back at Southside, Winnie and I were received and allowed to be in leadership roles. One that I became a part of was on a building committee. The church went through a pastoral problem during this time. The building committee was downsized by the withdrawal of some individuals from the church, but I still felt I was acting to the best of my ability on the committee. One of the things that bothered me to a degree was that when the building was constructed, the foundation was lower than some of the land immediately behind the building. Since we sometimes experienced unusually large rainfalls, there could be flooding of the church building. I thought it prudent to approach this problem prior to consideration for a building project.

I hired a man from Groves, who was with the city, to come and study the situation. He gave me a plan for the installation of drainage to the city outfall drain. I presented my findings to the remaining committee members and the pastor. This did not seem to be a prudent consideration for the committee, but I felt I had fulfilled my duty. Some, I believe, thought I became upset or angry because the church felt different than I, but that was not true. I felt I had filled my obligation, and during this time I served to find a new parsonage, and that worked out as a good thing for the church.

Seems I go from one thing to another quite often, and it happened here. Soon I found a place called Calvary Chapel in Beaumont that needed a music person. It was a mission project of Calvary Baptist Church in Beaumont and was located a little west of downtown Beaumont on a main thoroughfare in a deteriorating part of town. I used some of the music and educational skills I had acquired. Again, this was a situation where working with music was difficult. It was one thing to try to sing for worship, but it was another to have someone to play the piano. I was really sorry the experience ended the way it did. The young man who had been sent by the church to be pastor informed me of his music planning. My thought was that you can't have two people planning any program, so I sought other worship venues.

We had reached a point in our church experiences that was difficult, to say the least. Our denomination, the Southern Baptist Convention, was embroiled with a takeover by the fundamentalist arm of the convention. This bothered us. It involved the Baptist General Convention of Texas, which most churches supported. Winnie had tried to talk to her pastor, and he did not want to express any feelings along those lines, and I had no close affiliation at this point except trying to keep abreast through reading and attending conventions. With this as a background, Winnie and I decided it was time that we seek a place of worship and not be involved to any degree. I had visited a church in Beaumont, Calder Baptist, several times, and we decided to visit together.

We found after a short time and after a visit with a deacon and the interim pastor that this church seemed to offer what we needed. Remember, one of the things we were not going to do was get involved too deeply. Before long Winnie was teaching a class of women and had found a place where she not only could teach but also inspire a togetherness of sharing that endeared the women to her. In the meantime I had become involved with a mission project of ministering at retirement facilities and continued to do so for 15 years. From this place we served on many committees and groups.

While we were at Calder, we both served at the Baptist General Convention of Texas in important positions. I was the first to serve. Someone inquired of me if I would consider being nominated to a convention committee that searched out and presented to the convention persons to serve on the convention's executive committee. I was to present names for those in the lower East Texas area. I was elected and served the one-year term (all you were allowed to serve). While on this committee, I nominated a woman minister from Calder Church to be on the executive board, and she was elected. Later, she came to Winnie and asked if she would consider serving on the missions commission for the convention. Winnie agreed to have her name placed in nomination, and she was elected and served six years. So much for just going to church!

One thing I learned about churches over the years is that you can become involved easily. One rewarding observation I can make about our decision to go to Calder is the fact that through Winnie's involvement in the last years of her life was, she felt she really made a difference in the teaching and ministry of her class. These were her closest relationships since her youth years at First Baptist in Beeville.

I have described a little of my church life down through the years. Winnie came into my life, and we journeyed together, to be joined later by you. The church is and should be an important part of everyone's life after the experience of becoming a Christian.

49 Christmas Time

It's Christmas again! I have to admit that Christmas time is not my favorite time of year. I believe for a long time I have experienced a depression internally during Christmas. This is not because of what Christmas is all about. The baby's birth story from the Bible is one of the most important biblical stories recorded and, in this instance, celebrated. As a matter of fact, the last 20 or so years have made me more aware of the importance of Christmas to the Christian world.

I was brought up in a belief atmosphere that emphasized evangelism in worship rather than church service as a worship experience. In the early 1990s Winnie and I joined Calder Baptist Church and experienced a somewhat different approach to Christmas and Easter. The two of us had not been in fellowships of our denomination that emphasized Advent and Lenten periods, so we were blessed by these worship experiences. I say this as an indication that my religious practice does not come as a part of my wrestling with Christmastime.

As you know, my emotions do not show themselves very much in a visible display. All the joy and enthusiasm of Christmas has somewhat bypassed me. I believe this is a long-time part of my being.

I don't remember Christmas as being a great part of my childhood. This was because of the times in which we lived and the hand-to-mouth economy we as a family dealt with.

Later, as I managed the variety store, we started Christmas promotion, layaway, in July and thereby emphasized Christmas for six months of every year. By the time I reached Christmas, to tell the truth, I was exhausted and sometimes further exhausted by a lengthy drive home. "I'll be home for Christmas" has a different connotation when celebrated in this manner.

After Winnie and I married, I believe, this still existed with me. Shopping and gift choosing were depressing to me. I enjoy seeing people in a festive mood during the Christmas season, but I seem not turned in that fashion. I am glad we have these celebratory times with our friends and acquaintances. I believe it brings out the best in a lot of people when peace, joy, hope, and love are celebrated.

For a few days I will not be the best, but time will have passed and internal thoughts and external experiences will replace the negativity of the season.

Harold Brown Writes*

COUNTERACTION

A Cause to Fear

Fear is a dreadful thing. It is of the mind, but it is a child of the realties that surround the person. Fear of the dark is a prevalent thing among us human beings. Not that the dark will in itself be of harm to us, but because of the association of the violence and unknown that is a part of the dark.

Franklin Roosevelt, in his first inaugural address, boldly stated, "The only thing we have to fear is fear itself." With this simple phrase he was stating that the American people must have the faith in their own capacity to control their destiny.

Are we losing this capacity? Within the past few years the doubts that we hear expressed may well make us wonder. We doubt the security of our economic condition, although we live in an era of unprecedented wealth. We doubt the military capacity of our armed forces, although we have the best-equipped and best-manned force in history. We doubt the effectiveness and productivity of our space program, yet it is better planned and more widely known than any other in existence. Yes, we doubt, and doubt is the first step toward all-out fear.

Why should we have a cause to fear? Possibly one reason these fears have become evident is that our political atmosphere has naturally leaned toward fear. We hear so often the phrase, "I am afraid the government will do this, will not do that, will find out. I am afraid." It is though government has become associated with fear.

There is one thing to think upon. A little darkness is not as fearsome as a total darkness. Maybe if we had a little less government intervention in everything, there would be a little less cause to fear.

50 Adventures with Jim

My nephew, Jim, is a talented and adventurous person. He was born into the world as such. He arrived into the world, as I have written, at the coldest time I can remember. I have to recall a couple adventures I shared with him.

Jim invited me to go fishing with him at a place I had never visited and will probably never return. It was down in a bayou somewhere south of Bridge City, Texas, but that is getting ahead of the story.

Jim had acquired an aluminum boat, motor, and trailer. As I remember, the boat was a 12- or 14-footer. We had gathered up our fishing gear and proceeded to a launching place across the big bridge and in Bridge City.

I don't remember the exact way the boat was launched, but it was done quickly, and we boarded to start our journey to the fishing spot. As the motor fired up and Jim maneuvered the boat to begin the run, an unusual thing happened.

Somewhere between my legs or very close by, a small stream of water began to shoot up a foot or so in height. One of the rivets holding the seat structure to the boat had popped out. I don't remember how Jim came to know about this, but it was probably because I was making some kind of panicky noise.

Jim is very resourceful, and he did not let a little thing like a leak in the boat interfere with a good fishing trip. He shut the motor down and began searching through the tackle box he had brought along. Very quickly, he came to a solution to our leaky problem. One of his fishing lines had a bobber with a pointed wood pin running through it. Jim took the pin from the bobber and inserted it into the hole in the aluminum where the rivet had once been. Fortunately, it was just the right size, so a couple taps secured it, and the leak was stopped.

Merrily, we again set out on our fishing trip, which entailed a run down what I remember as Black's Bayou. We were skimming along with the aluminum boat riding high in the water with only an occasional slap of water caused by the crossing of small wavelets.

Off in the distance, I could see another boat. This bayou was also used by crew boats that serviced the offshore oil rigs. From my viewpoint that crew boat was quite anxious to get home.

To get this view in proper perspective, you must understand this bayou is 50 to 75 yards wide (that's my remembrance) and is bordered on each side by banks that seemed to be 8 to 10 feet in height. This crew boat approaching was running at pretty close to full speed. These boats are well-powered, and the wake (the wave created by the boat and motor) seemed to be just about the same height as the bordering banks. As you sit in a small aluminum boat, you have a thought that if you ride this wake out, you will either be inundated or if not will be thrown up on the bank.

Things worked out not all that bad. The crew boat cut its power and passed us by before again going to full power. We again proceeded to the fishing place. To get to the fishing place, we actually had to drag the boat over a small neck of land, but there we found a peaceful fishing place. Don't remember us catching a lot of fish, but you can see that venturing out with Jim could be quite exciting.

My next adventure with Jim was to accompany him on a duck-hunting trip down to Keith Lake and its surroundings. We again ventured forth in an aluminum boat, probably the same one with rivets now secure. We motored across the lake and soon beached the boat and dragged it across a small segment of land. We then launched the boat in a long, narrow canal and began to run for some length of time. Jim determined the proper place to stop, and we secured the boat and made our way to hunt. I do not remember what success we had in the hunt, but it had come time for us to start on our way back.

All aboard, game and gear secure, we shoved away from the bank. The motor fired up easily, but we didn't move! Jim cut the motor and raised it so the propeller was visible. After a little inspection he informed me there was a sheared pin. No problem, he assured me, as he always had extra pins stored in the motor cowling. He lifted the cover; the place where the pins were stored was vacant. Seems he had loaned the boat earlier, and the borrowers must have had a sheared pin problem also.

Using the anchor lines and other ropes, we made our way along the canal, towing the boat and its load of gear. We reached the land neck crossing into Keith Lake but saw no boating activity. Jim began to busily search the area around the landing place. There had been a trapper's shack here at one time, but it had burned.

Jim's searching did turn up some interesting items: He found a couple somewhat rusty and burn-heated nails. Also, he found an old knife blade. Using the knife blade as a cutting force and a couple bricks for surface, Jim managed to cut two makeshift pins. He was able to get them so they would fit the propeller's shaft opening. With one of the pins in place and a spare in reserve, Jim fired up the motor, and off we went.

Again, we had made it home safely, and Jim had given me a couple adventurous remembrances to tell a couple times and even now record.

51 Hitching a Ride with Don

Coming through a holiday period reminded me of a holiday experience while in the Air Force at Keesler Field in Biloxi, Mississippi. Don, a fellow airman, and myself had determined to take a hitchhiking trip over a long weekend. He was from Massachusetts and had never been to Texas except for his basic training. We were going to visit Malakoff.

As I remember, it was a Fourth of July weekend that we planned to make the trip. We could leave on Friday after our classes. Then we would have Saturday, Sunday, and Monday to make the trip, have a couple days in Malakoff, and return for duty on Tuesday. Our plans got sidetracked when someone (I suppose it was the base commander) called for a Saturday morning formation and parade so the troops could be reviewed. This meant we could not depart until about noon on Saturday.

Hitchhiking in those days was a pretty good way for GIs to travel, and we made it to Shreveport, Louisiana, by about midnight. We made our way to the outskirts of Shreveport and proceeded to seek further transportation. We had not long to wait. A man and a woman stopped and offered us a ride with the indication they were going for quite a distance. I believe the car was a Ford two-door sedan. It was to be a memorable ride.

We had hardly got seated, in the back of course, when the driver started out down the dark and crooked road, headed toward Texas. There was some conversation, and I believe Don and I felt quite safe and knew we were making good travel time as the driver set a pretty heavy foot to the pedal.

Now, it wasn't long before the driver, or perhaps it was the woman, produced a clear fruit jar that passed between the two for a shared sip. They were a cordial couple, so they invited Don and me to share. I believe what the jar contained was called "salty dog," which I remember as gin mixed with grapefruit juice or something similar. At that time my Baptist leanings were still intact, so I passed the jar to Don, and he sampled the contents.

As we progressed, I believe both Don and I felt that our speed was increasing and a party-like atmosphere was beginning to show in the driver and his companion. It was not long until the jar was passed again. It seems Don was a little more serious in how much he sampled. This scene may have occurred a time or two more, and I think Don and I had become a little concerned about our safety as we hurled through the dark Louisiana night on the two-lane curved highway.

I suppose our concern became obvious to the driver and his companion after a time. They began to have a good laugh. They had scared the "begibbers" out of two Air Force hitchhikers.

The driver and his companion had come from the base on the outskirts of Shreveport and were on their way to Wichita Falls, Texas. As I remember, he was a club bartender on the base. I think we determined that most of the salty dog had been drunk by Don as it was passed around. The couple knew they had a long night's travel to get to Wichita Falls.

We ended our travel with the couple at Gladewater and continued our travels toward Malakoff. We thanked them for the exciting ride and bid them safe travel.

This was the exciting part of our weekend travels, as I don't think Don was too impressed with Malakoff and he really didn't get to meet too many people, especially girls. He had been raised in Denham, Massachusetts, a suburb of Boston, so Texas was different. We did not arrive in Malakoff until up in the day Sunday and were rather tired. Of course, the return journey had to begin on Monday.

As I think back, I still marvel at the goodness of people who gave GIs rides all over the land. Don and I had been participants in this grand adventure because of them.

52 Daddy's Demise

I have written a little about my father, Daddy, but I probably have never explained or talked too much about his illness and finally his death. He died on April 10, 1956, so you didn't ever get to know him.

When I left home for the Air Force, Daddy was still finding and performing work as a carpenter. I do not remember when the family was first alerted to the fact that something was occurring with him. It is my recollection that it was Tom Johnson who came to Robbie, my brother, and indicated something was not right with Daddy.

"Uncle Tom," as we knew him, had been raised in Cayuga at the same time as Daddy, so they had known each other since childhood. After they married and had children, they both settled in Malakoff. I can remember in our early days at Malakoff that Uncle Tom and Aunt Johnnie had a storm cellar, which was actually a hole in the red clay hill with a roof over it and an entry door. We did not have a cellar, so on a couple occasions we shared their cellar.

Both Daddy and Uncle Tom had the same occupation. This is why Uncle Tom came to Robbie. As I remember, Uncle Tom had a job in Trinidad that required another carpenter, and he had hired Daddy to fill the position. His explanation in coming to Robbie was that he fairly well knew Daddy, and something was occurring that was out of character for Daddy. Uncle Tom would assign a job to Daddy, and when he would come back later to check on the progress, Daddy would be involved in something else. Daddy would not have normally left a job assignment without talking to the person running the job. This was our first indication that something was wrong.

As time went by (I have to tell this from my understanding because I was away in the Air Force), Daddy began to wander off from home and get lost. I don't remember how long from Uncle Tom's timely warning until Daddy became a real problem to Grandmamma and Robbie. I think it also became a concern for other friends.

Sometime later, Edith and I came to visit in Malakoff and were made more aware of the situation. She lived in Port Neches and by this time was managing a variety store in Groves. Of course, I was in the Air Force at Ellington Field in Houston.

Edith and I departed Malakoff, and as we talked and discussed the situation about Daddy, we became concerned to the point we returned to Malakoff. I think we had gotten as far as Palestine. On our return we made arrangements so we could stay over for a time. I worked with a family friend, actually Uncle Tom's son-in-law, who worked in the county courthouse and assisted veterans, I believe. He was able to work through the Red Cross and obtain an emergency leave for me.

I don't remember the details, but we somehow learned that a person with mental problems could be placed in a state institution for six months for treatment and/or evaluation. This had to done through the county judge and would be temporary.

This seems odd in the day in which we live now, but back in the 1940s and 1950s there were very few places, if any, like a retirement home. The Odd Fellows and Masons had homes, but they were not for this type of evaluation or treatment. What made this situation and internment seem harsh was that the institution was a state asylum. This institution was in Terrell, Texas. Of course, our commitment of Daddy to this institution quickly spread to the external family members. It is my understanding that one of Daddy's sister was really upset and upbraided Robbie at some point.

The first commitment, as I stated, was for six months. Brother Robbie, and I presume his wife, Maxine, picked up Daddy on his release. It is my understanding that Robbie remembered the upbraiding, so instead of taking Daddy home, he just drove down to Cayuga to the home of the disturbed sister and left Daddy with her.

The above situation did not last long; the sister contacted Robbie to make other arrangements and pick Daddy up. Daddy's condition was such that no one in the family was in a position to take care of Daddy's needs. The first commitment was for six months; the second would be for permanent care.

I visited Daddy a few times in the asylum at Terrell. His mental condition had been diagnosed as "hardening of the arteries." His arteries along each side of his neck were becoming clogged with plaque. This dreadful condition led to Daddy gradually digressing through his earlier life to infancy. The last time I saw him prior to this accident causing his demise, he spoke to me as if I were his brother, Minor Brown.

I believe it was on April 9, 1956, that the general manager of the variety stores came to West Columbia and told me Daddy had had an accident and was in critical condition. I arranged to pick up Edith, and we made our way to Malakoff and subsequently to the hospital in Terrell. Grandmamma, Robbie, and Maxine either were there or had been there during the day. Edith and I determined we should stay the night, and the others returned home. It was a rather long night.

At various intervals it seemed Daddy would be stressed to the edge of death. The attendants, as I remember, would give him a shot or something that caused him to relax. I believe this happened several times during the night. Daddy finally expired at about 5:00 AM on April 10.. Edith and I, as we drove back to Malakoff, questioned why the attendants seemed to prolong the death of one whose body and mind had so deteriorated. Of course, years later, we know that this seems to happen with new procedures where artificial means can seem to prolong life.

Sometimes I question or feel some sense of guilt in that I have lived so long and enjoyed such an eventful and fruitful lifestyle while one who worked and labored so hard and suffered such indignity never enjoyed that part of life. I still marvel at his dedication to his family and the provisions he made to the best of his ability (note: What happened to Daddy, the clogging of the arteries, also happened to Mom Harris, but by the time hers occurred, the surgeons were able to operate and remove the buildup from her arteries with success).

53 A Floundering Trip

From about August 1958 until November 1960 we lived in Corpus Christi. Not only did we find ourselves in Corpus, but Pop and Mom had moved there also. Winnie's sister, Helen, her husband, Alva, and their two children had lived there for some time. We enjoyed having the family around.

Corpus Christi and the surrounding area are widely known for the many opportunities afforded anyone wishing to fish. Among the many fish that inhabit the bays and inlets is the flounder. Flounder may be fished with bait and hook, but a popular method of getting flounder along the lower Gulf is by "gigging." Gigging takes place in the dark of the night by wading along in the shallows of the bays and inlets with a bright light. The flounder lies flat in or on the sandy bottom, and by shining the light toward the water, they become visible. The gig is a pronged fork mounted on a pole, and when the flounder is located, it is immediately impaled on the gig by driving the forked gig into its body. The flounder can then be prepared and broiled for a delectable dinner.

Pop, Alva, and I got together after hearing and reading about the success people were having in floundering around the area and planned to go flounder gigging. Copano Bay, near Rockport, seemed to have been a hot spot, so we selected it as the site for us to go on a Friday night and try our hand at gigging some flounders.

Equipment-wise we were a little short, as I remember. Alva may have had a gig, and all of us had shoes we used to wear to the beach, but the problem was the light. Alva worked at the highway department, and I believe that is where he borrowed a gas lantern. The Friday night came, and we piled into Pop's faithful Plymouth car, which had just been outfitted with new seat covers.

On arrival at the bay-front area, the attempt was made to light the lantern, using the car's headlights to see. I believe you had to pump a little pressure into the lantern fuel tank to start the fuel flow. No luck, so it was determined that we should go back into town where there were some streetlights. Back into the Plymouth we went and made the trip back to Rockport. In a short while success was achieved, and the lantern burned brightly. A concern developed about turning the lantern off. Would we be able to relight it when we got back to the beach? A decision was made to turn it down very low and place it on the floorboard between front and back seat. As I remember, Alva was riding in the back.

Now, if there anything South Texas men enjoy when hunting and fishing, it is stopping in the local restaurant for a cup of coffee. It was Pop's suggestion, and he was driving, so we went to a well-known restaurant in Rockport. I have said that this was taking place on a Friday night. There were other things that occurred on Friday night in South Texas; I believe in this instance it was a football game. The parking was limited, but we found a spot, and then another problem arose. We had this lighted lantern in the car. Another decision was made, and Alva was to stay with the car and lantern; Pop and I would bring him coffee. Everyone had his coffee, and we were off to the bay again.

The lantern was working fine, and we made our way back to the bay shore. As we piled out of the car, we noticed the wind had begun to blow. Wading shoes on, gig at the ready, lantern turned to give the brightest light, we waded into the surf. It wasn't long before we determined the wind was not only blowing our headwear and hair, but it had stirred the water. What happens to the water on a sandy beach when it is stirred? Remember the idea was to see the flounder and gig it before it could swim away. The water had become so stirred and murky that we could not see anything on the bottom. No floundering.

We returned to the car and turned off the lantern, rather disheartened. Pop was probably the one who was the most disheartened. Trying to keep that lantern lit by placing it in the back between the seats was a huge mistake. I mentioned that Pop had just bought new seat covers for his car. Now there was a strip of melted plastic about 4 inches wide and 15 or so inches long up the back of that seat cover.

I don't recall ever having another discussion about flounder fishing after this incident.

54 Mrs. Blackwell

You will remember when the three of us left the Southside Church and moved to the First Baptist Church in Port Neches. Shortly after that move, I became involved with a mission project of the church that was located at the low-rent housing project, Woodcrest. The Woodcrest facility had some interesting facets in its history.

The Woodcrest development had been constructed during WWII to supply housing for the workers at Neches Butane and the tire companies located there. Neches Butane produced a product that could be used as a synthetic rubber for automobile tires. Woodcrest had suffered some deterioration and had become a low-rent apartment facility.

Mrs. Blackwell and her family lived in Woodcrest and were an important part of the worship and teaching ministry of the mission. Mr. Blackwell had physical problems that kept him from working, so Mrs. Blackwell contributed to the family's economy by working at a small drive-in grocery in the area.

One of the problems in mission efforts such as this is having people with needed talents volunteer and then withdraw. Such was the problem at Woodcrest in having a pianist for worship and other activities. At times a woman would volunteer and come to be the pianist. Everyone would be blessed by her talents and presence, but after a short time, it seemed, other things became more important: the husband who didn't like attending church by himself or the woman missing being part of the church's worship and activities.

At times a teenage pianist would be drawn to serve with their talent. Then things would happen: like a parent was concerned because of the area in which the mission was located or the youngster missed being part of the big church's youth activities. Things like this go with the territory, so to speak.

After a few aforementioned situations occurred, Mrs. Blackwell came to me, as I was the music director for the mission. She explained that in her younger years, she had been able to play the piano, but she said she played "by ear." This meant she did not read music but rather had a talent of playing or performing on the piano by hearing and reproducing music she had heard.

Mrs. Blackwell told me, "Mr. Brown, if you will help me by showing me where on the keyboard the notes for the song are located and what the melody is, I believe I might be able to play some of the hymns."

I began to show her where to start, and using well-known hymns, we would plan music for the Sunday worship service. Her family acted as maintenance persons for the mission, so she had a key, which allowed her to use the mission piano for practice. Later, Mrs. Blackwell purchased a piano for her apartment and used it for family entertainment as well as for her hymn practice. She really liked to play.

As a side note to Mrs. Blackwell's story, I must comment on how God has blessed some persons with unusual music abilities and talent but they did not or have not had the benefit of formal instruction and opportunity of training for their instrument or voice. Unfortunately, at times educated musicians fail to recognize raw talent.

Over a period of years, Mrs. Blackwell became able to play a large number of hymns from the Baptist hymnal and, as an added blessing, many popular and old-time gospel songs. She and her family had a background in gospel music, so it was a special blessing for them. Mrs. Blackwell's daughter would sing the lead (soprano), a teenager who lived with the Blackwells sang alto, and a Blackwell son sang the tenor part. They let me sing along in a bass part. We occasionally used this in our worship music. It was an energizer for the Blackwell family as well as for me.

I guess we were a little prideful in our performance as a quartet and she as the pianist, because we actually did a couple concerts: one at a Baptist church in West Orange and another at a Baptist church in Sabine Pass. I'm not sure, but we may have sung at the First Baptist in Port Neches. I know Mrs. Blackwell played for me a time or two there.

Mrs. Blackwell is no longer with us, but I'm sure that when she reached her heavenly reward, there must have been a place for her to share her musical talents. I believe if there are not pianos in heaven, she could have mastered the harp rather easily.

55 Apples

To begin with, the trip was going to be interesting and a little exciting. Winnie and I had scheduled two Elderhostels (Road Scholar) in Georgia, one quickly followed the next week by a second one. We had attended these before but never in this manner. We knew that after the second Elderhostel, we would travel back to Texas over a weekend and go to Dallas for a Mission Commission meeting. Winnie served the Baptist General Convention of Texas on this commission for six years.

Our first Elderhostel was at a place just north of Atlanta. As I remember, it was sponsored by a college in Kennesaw. I don't remember the topics covered by this Elderhostel, but it was for a week's stay. At the end of the week, on Saturday morning, we checked out and had a weekend to travel and spend before the check-in on Sunday at the next Elderhostel in Toccoa, Georgia, in the northeastern region of the state.

Since we had some time to drive to Toccoa, we chose to travel to the northern region of Georgia and see the activities there. One of the places we visited was Ellijay. One of the things we discovered was that this region produced a lot of apples. After a stop or two and some conversations, I learned apples could be kept almost indefinitely if kept cool, in the 40- to 50-degree range, as I remember. This trip was in fall, and the night temperatures were in that range. I believe I finally selected a bushel of apples. They could travel with us, and we could enjoy some and share some when we got back to Texas at Malakoff on our way to Dallas.

We arrived in Toccoa at the appointed time on Sunday afternoon. The temperature had not been hot, and I had kept ice around the apples. The night was to be cool, so I made sure the car windows were open a little to allow the night's coolness to flow into the car. For seven days and nights I alternated, taking ice out to the car early in the morning and going in the evening and opening the windows for the coolness of the night to creep in.

Everything was working fine, and the apples were in good condition on arrival in Malakoff on the next Sunday. Since we had to be in Dallas (I believe it was on Monday and the weather was fairly cool), I stored the apples in my sister Edith's garage. Edith's husband, Arvel, was in a nursing home.

Winnie and I made our trip to Dallas for her meeting and arrived back in Malakoff to an unexpected situation: Arvel had passed away, and Edith was faced with the preparation for his funeral. As long as the weather was cool, the apples were fine.

I don't remember the number of days before the funeral and interment took place, but somewhere in time one of those blue Texas northers came whistling down the pike. Now I was faced with a new problem: the apples needed to be cool but not frozen. I had to be sure they were protected from the cold.

As a side note I must say that this was undoubtedly the coldest funeral I ever attended. The interment was at a cemetery out the Tyler highway, east of Athens, on a hillside. Edith and Arvel's family had arranged for him to be buried next to his first wife. I believe this pleased his children.

We finally arrived home after this eventful trip with apples in tow. After caring for those apples for the better part of two weeks, I think I may have lost some of my taste for apples. I view them in the grocery store—it used to be delicious, maybe one or two more, were the apples from which you selected; now there must be 15 or 20 kinds, some from as far away as Australia.

I remember they must be kept cool!

56 Rubber Guns

"Rubber gun" does not mean a gun or gun-like object made out of rubber. I'll get to that.

I see on television and hear on the radio about young children being punished for making a drawing that looks like a gun, or I believe in one instance a child had folded his three fingers into the palm of his hand and pointed the forefinger to form a gun-like appearance, and this called for the child to be expelled from school. The persons behind such rulings would not have been able to live during the years of my early childhood.

The most common type of play gun of my early childhood was the cap pistol, a small metal pistol-like toy in which one cap (a paper that contained powder that popped when struck) could be placed and fired. Others were more elaborate toy guns; sometimes they came in pairs with a belt and scabbard, and they fired rolled caps. I suppose some could fire as many as 50 caps without stopping. This may have been taken up by some of the cowboy movies where seemingly countless shots could be fired from a six-shooter.

As I remember, there was one very expensive gun that actually had a round set of caps that fit on a cylinder much like a real six-shooter. I think my caps were like the rolled ones that could be purchased for a nickel and the box contained about five rolls. (This is not what I started to write about!)

Most of the time we did not have a lot of store-bought toys. We had to improvise. One kind of toy gun we could make from a few pieces of scrap was the "rubber gun." Collect a 12- or 15-inch scrap of lumber for a pistol or a 3-foot scrap for a rifle and add an old inner tube, a clothes pin, and a length of cord or strap of leather, and we were equipped to make a firearm (rubber gun).

Pistol: Neil and I were fortunate on these guns because Daddy was a carpenter, so there were always scraps around, and Daddy had saws. A small piece of lumber could be sawed to resemble a pistol with a small notch at the barrel end and either a slant- or 90-degree-angled hand grip. Which did you want to be: a cowboy or a detective? The clothes pin would then be attached to the hand grip using string or cord wrapping so the clothes pin opening was up. Clothes pins could also be mounted with small nails. The inner tube would be cut into 3/8-inch-wide strips and about the length of the wood pistol. The two ends of the length of rubber would now be inserted into the clothes pin and the formed loop drawn out to the notch end of the pistol. You were now loaded and ready for robber or outlaw.

Rifle: The rifle-like wooden gun was also sawed to a general form of a rifle with a notch at the end of the barrel. At the armrest end of the barrel, a one-inch cut down to the armrest and with the armrest to one's liking. On the barrel just in in front of the one-inch cut would be about six or so notches. On the barrel end in front of the notches, a cord or leather strap would be securely attached. Ready for loading! Your rifle had to be long enough to accommodate the inner tube you had. Narrow strips of the tube would be cut across the tube so you had a circle of rubber. To load the rifle one would place the circle of rubber into the barrel-end notch and stretch it back to the notches close to the armrest, making sure the cord or leather strip would be underneath. All the rubber bands would be loaded and ready for battle! To fire your rifle all you had to do was pull on the cord or leather strip and the rubber bands would be on their way to leave a welt if they found bare skin.

Other toys were made: slingshots; scooters out of skates, hoops, or small discarded metal wheels steered by a stick with a U-shaped tobacco can attached as a guide. I remember being rolled around in old discarded automobile ties. Guess I am one of those who survived without being disabled, dismembered, or blinded. We did have fun with what we had to play with in spite of bruises, aches, and pains.

57 Pop's Barbeque

You will remember a lot about this. First, you will recognize there are two distinct things related to Pop's barbeque. One is the barbeque sauce. You memorialized this in Frankie Martin's and Ida Schario's "Family Favorites" cookbook on page 106. I note there have been a few side notes diminishing the recipe size, such as one small bottle of Louisiana hot sauce reduced to a quarter of a bottle and six lemons reduced to two. Do you remember the original recipe was for 100 pounds of meat?

There is another of Pop's barbeque contributions that I want to remind you about. Pop and Mom had moved to Corpus Christi to live after he had found a job. Pop got the idea that there should be a good barbeque cooking place, as he liked to occasionally prepare his delicious barbeque. Helen and Alva lived in

Corpus and had purchased a home in a fairly nice neighborhood. Since Helen and Alva had a good-sized backyard, this would be a good place for a permanent location, and he would build it to his own design.

I will have to estimate the dimensions (if you want to check them out, I believe you might visit that old address). He had a local someone to use red brick to construct a rectangle about 6 feet long, 3 feet wide, and 24 or so inches in height. It had an inside metal support that the meat could be laid on. At one end there was a small fire box where mesquite wood could be placed and burned. At the other end there was a pipe sticking up and, as I remember, an attached lid that could be used to control the airflow through the fire box, the cooking area, and out of the pipe. The cooking area was probably two feet by four feet; it was made to cook about 100 pounds of meat. The pit had a sheet-iron cover that was counterweighted and covered the top opening. The pit was to be used with a small fire to produce a lot of heat and a little smoke for 10 or 12 hours of cooking. I have failed to mention that it was constructed on a concrete pad with a little extension around it. He had the best barbeque pit in town!

Now, there was a problem that arose a little while later. Helen and Alva divorced, and Helen moved off to another end of town and remarried. This created a perplexing problem, but Pop had a solution. After Helen got settled into a new place, Pop arranged for someone to go to Alva's backyard, load up the barbeque pit, and move it to a new location in Helen's backyard. Pop was back in the barbeque business, and he had the best barbeque pit in town.

A very sad thing occurred along the way. Helen had a sudden illness and died. The situation with her marriage at this time I do not recall, but we do know the barbeque pit had to be dealt with.

Alva and the two children were living at the old home site of the barbeque pit. Pop and Mom had not purchased a home and lot in Corpus, so there was only one thing to do. Pop again got someone to go and load up the barbeque pit and move it back to the original site.

I guess in telling this story, which I'm sure you remember parts of, I am reminding you of how resourceful your grandfather was. This is just one instance that illustrates how he attacked a problem, and if anything went awry, he would adjust and continue to some end.

58 The 3rd Grade

I doubt I ever talked to you much about an illness I had when I was young; it was rheumatic fever, which occurs usually in youngsters and most of the time after a strep throat infection. There are several symptoms: I had a fever, of course, but the most telling was the swelling and pains in the joints of my arms and legs. There are sometimes other symptoms, but these are the ones I remember. At times there is an aftereffect of the infection in that a heart valve can be damaged. I was fortunate to not have this occur. I did have my tonsils removed by Dr. Kilman; as I remember, this was somewhat a specialty of his.

I do not remember how much of third grade I missed, but it was most of it. Miss Edna Willis was the teacher, and I know she visited me at home, and I suppose she must have left books and information so I could study.

Daddy set up a bed in the living room, and I was mostly bedbound for several months. One of the things that kept me company and entertained me was the little brown radio. Not many third-graders knew about Ma Perkins, Pepper Young's Family, Guiding Light, and Young Widder Brown. Of course, they did know about Jack Armstrong, Little Orphan Annie, and the Lone Ranger. These kept me occupied during the day, by evening Lum and Abner, Amos and Andy, and Fibber McGee and Molly.

There was one that came on Sunday evening called *One Man's Family*. It was about a family in San Francisco, and the eldest son was named Paul, which may have fed into how you were named. Another one that was a daily program, I believe, and it was at 10:30 at night, was called *I Love a Mystery*. The opening of the show was a creaking door, and the stories were a little scary.

Having missed nearly all of third grade meant that when I returned the next year, I had to go back to third grade and Miss Willis. I must have studied more than I realized while I was out, because at the end of the first six weeks, they promoted me to be with Miss Jarvis's fourth-grade class. I managed to study and had pretty good grades all through school, even to high school.

The only other time the sickness interfered with me, except for all the reminders I got from Mama to not exert myself, was many years later after I had been in the Air Force for about three years. The Air Force determined I needed to have a physical examination; I suppose this was because I was on flying status. Part of the examination included questions about my medical background and previous illnesses. When I told them I had rheumatic fever as a child, all kinds of bells must have rang. I was slated for some additional tests. I told them about the rheumatic fever when I enlisted in the Air Force, and I had been on flying status for a couple years. Everything worked out, and I was cleared and continued to fly at least once a month (which I had to do to be paid flight pay). My enlistment was extended from three to four years because of the Korean conflict.

I believe I was exceptionally blessed by not having aftereffects from the rheumatic fever. Except for the collapsed lung I wrote about and a little depression, I have been blessed with good health. I can still make it around the block every morning if it's not too cold. I really don't like walking—all the things that pass through one's mind—but I suppose it is somewhat like meditation.

59 Being Political

Next to one's belief in God, there is the important aspect of life that is government and its support and following. My long-term understanding is that capitalism and conservatism have been the most beneficial form of government for humankind where practiced with the moral and ethical tenets of the Christian faith.

As a child the singularly controlled state of Texas by the Democratic Party, I suppose, had its influence. I say this because the only thing I can remember from childhood pertaining to the politics of the time was a little saying we kids repeated: "The horse's tail is long and silky; raise it up, and look at Willkie!" Wendell Willkie was an early 1940s Republican candidate against Roosevelt for president of the United States.

My first experience with the election of a president was in the early 1950s. I voted for Dwight Eisenhower. I believe what little understanding I had about politics was that the Republican Party was more attuned to my belief in what government should be. As time has gone by, I am more convinced by further understanding and application. I think one of the determining factors was the observation of what had been the complete domination of the Democratic

Party in Texas and some of its practices that were against what the country had been founded on.

As I remember, I voted but otherwise did not have much political drive or participation until the 1960s. I then had an opportunity and understanding to try to participate in the political process.

We had moved to Port Neches in 1960, and it had become quite evident that the Golden Triangle, formed by Beaumont, Orange, and Port Arthur, was one of the most solid Democratic areas of the state of Texas. The precinct in which we lived had only a few that voted in the Republican primary, although the general elections showed a little more Republican support.

As I recall, my first entry as a participant in the political realm, other than as a voter, came in 1962. Of course, Winnie had been involved in Pop's running for two or three political positions in Bee County. I believe the precinct needed a place for the Republicans to vote in the primary, and by some determination that election was held in our home on Combs Drive. Only a few voted in the Republican primary because all the local race choices were in the Democratic primary. We did not receive compensation for this as there was no pay for being a clerk or election judge.

When we got to 1964, I made my first and last venture into elected politics by being listed for the position of precinct chairman. I believe this came about because a person who had previously held this position was moving away or was incapacitated. Very few people voted, but I was elected! I understood that now I was to represent the 38th precinct at the meetings of the county Republicans. I was the most ignorant of all politicians. I presumed I would be notified, where and when, of meetings of the county Republicans.

Again, as I recall, several months went by, and I had no notification of meetings. One day at the plant where I worked, another person who was a precinct chairman asked me why I had not been attending the county meetings. Of course, I responded that I was unaware of meetings because no one had notified me about them. I believe he then pursued the question with the county organization.

A short time later Don, who was the other precinct chairman, advised me I was not a viable chairman. It seems that the precinct lines had been changed, and this voided my election.

I have thought about this occasionally since this happened. Jefferson County did not have a lot of persons who were willing to give up their primary voting privilege. I had. The question then becomes why the county chairman had not made an effort to have me appointed to fill the vacancy. I'm sure there was a way it could have been done. I have a theory of why.

During the previous election a doctor from Bridge City had run for the position of U.S. House of Representatives for our area. He was in the race against the long-time representative Jack Brooks from Beaumont. The Republicans of Jefferson County did not support the doctor. I had helped a little by promoting the doctor in precinct 38. I distributed campaign literature door-to-door. We may have even sent the doctor a few dollars for support. Let me explain something.

Jack Brooks was second only to Lyndon Johnson in political smarts. He would make all the union halls in the area in his electioneering and the next day be at the Chamber of Commerce dinner in Beaumont asking for their support. In Congress he represented the unions and obtained money for Lamar University and the Jefferson County airport. Who would not support him?

I believe the county chairman just may have taken this into consideration in my case. After all, I had supported someone who opposed the incumbent, though from the other party had done good for the area. Since my election had been voided, he chose not to invite me to fill the position. You don't bite the hand that feeds you. In some ways the representative, although from a different party, filled the needs of the area. To be honest I didn't like the county chairman, as he was an authoritarian individual who seemed to rule with a heavy hand.

I have remained a Republican through the years, as the state of Texas has found a lot of support and elected a good many Republicans to state offices, and even a few locally. I feel like conservatism, as it relates to the Constitution, and capitalism is the best way of government.

My age group has been blessed with the most scientific and technological advantages of all history, in spite of having to sacrifice some to keep the world safe. My hope is that somehow there can be a continuance of these blessings for the generations that follow us.

Harold Brown Writes*

COUNTERACTION

Slow Horses

It is rather evident by some of the things we read and hear today that anyone who is concerned about the political and economic life of the United States and speaks out in the attitude of "let us proceed with all caution" is immediately labeled a "slow horse," a radical if you please.

Most of us want all the problems of our nation solved immediately. Spend some more money, but get the job done. Make a law to cover the immediate danger, and history be hanged. Establish a policy of administration with ethics forgotten. Run like a racehorse for one big prize.

I would like to submit to you that all horses are not racehorses. I ran across a statement that deserves some thought: "Don't abuse the slow horse. Maybe it was intended to pull heavy loads." I really think that a workhorse is a good thing to have around to do a big job.

Certainly our nation is faced with some of the most critical problems of our history. Some of the problems that we have were present from the beginning and more than likely will continue for inestimable periods of time. Other problems that we have are transitional in nature and must be approached with the utmost caution, because the very nature of change is toward an unknown.

I am always leery of these "racehorse" politicians who seem to have an answer for each and every problem that arises. It seems that a good portion of our income is going to support some of these racehorses. Our law books are becoming full of statues completely foreign to our historical background. Where has ethics disappeared in the heap of policy making?

Hitching our wagon to a good workhorse might help pull the load as well as save the wagon from its wheels running off. Where is that "slow horse"?

60 The Ladies

This may be the most difficult subjects I will write about. As we leave childhood and move into the teenage years, there is the first of life's experiences. It moves from a protective family culture of moral and ethical teachings to the application of those teachings to those outside the family. One of the most important is the relationship with women in our lives.

I have been blessed with having women in my life who, as the saying goes, were "above my pay grade." Joanne was the first. I really don't know how we became important to one another in my junior year of high school. She was a senior and very popular in our small high school. I believe our closest link, to begin with, was the fact we were in first-year Spanish class and were both in the high school band.

In regard to the "pay grade," I was really above my social status in my relationship to her. She was from an old community family that was involved in extremely important businesses for Malakoff. Her grandmother was a published poet of some renown. I can also add that we were from different religious denominations: Methodist and Baptist.

My junior year found Joanne and I together in varied circumstances: Spanish class, the movies, sports events, and just hanging out. Our mode of transportation was to walk just about everywhere except when we double-dated with a couple that had a car. This was a war year. One shared experience was her senior play. Her class was a little short on male students, and the play that was chosen called for more than presented themselves for the roles. I got to sub for one of the minor parts. Another big sharing was her invitation for me to escort her to the junior-senior banquet.

This was my first experience of sharing a relationship outside the family. It was real to me and also to her, but about a year later I suggested that we abandon our close association. She was a student at Southern Methodist University as I finished high school. I have to admit I carried a torch for her for many years afterward.

Winnie and I had occasionally met Joanne at community reunions in Malakoff, so Joanne and Winnie got to meet each other and visit. A few weeks after Winnie had left us, I was in Fort Worth for a Baptist convention. Joanne lived in Fort Worth, and through a mutual friend I invited her and her husband to lunch. Still friends after all these years.

We can skip a number of years until my faithful circumstance of moving to West Columbia. Not long after moving there, I joined the First Baptist Church. I believe I had begun to sing with the choir when a woman approached me and confirmed that I was not married. After that determination that I was single, she informed me that I would not leave West Columbia without a bride. They would find me a wife. Little did I know!

I have written how our mutual friend, Harris, antagonized Winnie and me for a year. In September when Winnie returned to West Columbia for the start of school, I invited her out to a movie. If I remember, it was the latest Elvis Presley. I know we walked out of his movie at some place. This may have been an indication that we had similar thoughts, at least about movies.

It's a wonder Winnie stayed with me after the first year. We married, and quickly I had an opportunity to go to La Porte to open a variety store. She didn't miss a lick; she got a teaching job. Then we determined after a short time to get me some more education, which involved a move to Corpus Christi, where again she got a teaching job. While there in Corpus, Winnie and I were blessed with you, Paul, joining us. She was out of teaching for about one semester and then resumed teaching at midterm. Now, this was quite a change and accomplishment for a woman who once was determined to not be married. I believe I remember she had purchased silverware with the letter H engraved on them.

As I have indicated, I was way above my "pay grade" when considering the blessing of such a person as Winnie. She had come from a successful family background of politics and business. Winnie herself was successful; prior to our marriage, she had taught school for about eight or nine years. She was an excellent teacher and continued, as you know, until she had completed 31 years. Winnie then only retired because of her feet, which after years of standing were bad enough for the doctor to recommend retirement.

Over a considerable number of years, I marveled as Winnie dealt with some difficult physical problems, especially with her back. She was examined by doctors in Beaumont and Houston, supposedly the best, and all agreed that her bone density could not support a surgical brace. I know you will remember a little about this because she was in the hospital in Beaumont when you were thrown from the horse and broke your collarbone. For several years she also had a very painful situation with her knee. We were at a convention in Fort Worth, I believe, and we were making our way to the car when Winnie tripped and went down on her knee. Later, this had to be surgically dealt with but not corrected. In early 2008 a surgeon in Beaumont operated on her back, and it is my belief that she was relieved from her back pain for the first time in some 40-plus years.

Winnie and I had some differences, not unlike most married couples, over our 51-plus years together—most, if not all, a result of my wants or decisions. There is one decision I am most proud of, and it was made early on. We agreed she would take care of the checkbook. I thought she would be most comfortable with that decision, as she had been self-reliant before we married. That was one of the better decisions I ever made. It worked great!

Our religious values and training were very similar. After moving to Port Neches and over a great number of years, I became involved with a number of Baptist churches and/or missions, usually as music director. Winnie was always supportive in our moving from church to church. We both used our talents at Southside, First Baptist, Woodcrest (Port Arthur), and eventually Calder in Beaumont. We were going to Calder and retire. That didn't work very well, as we both found ourselves involved and happy to be part of that fellowship.

The last days Winnie and I shared together were both a blessing and a catastrophe. We had fled Port Neches to escape hurricane Ike. We had the blessing of staying at Janet's Bed and Breakfast in Malakoff. Paul, you and Tammie returned to Port Neches and determined we had no house damage but also found out the city water plant had extensive damage and it would not be a good idea for us to return just yet.

As time went by, I had a thought and shared it with Winnie, and she agreed. We had not visited Winnie's sister Kay and family for some time. Although Winnie was having some problem with her right knee, we would drive to Corpus Christi very leisurely. After checking with Kay, we set out and drove to Corpus. I believe the visit was delightful for Winnie and Kay. When we received the all-clear that the water plant worked again for Port Neches, we drove back to our home in Port Neches.

I cannot remember how long, but within a short time Winnie began to experience a loss of energy and difficulty moving around the house. It was a

Sunday morning when it became evident Winnie was needful of medical care. I had to help her from the bed into her wheelchair. I fixed breakfast and sought to carry her to the emergency room, but she suggested since I had prepared to do the service at Sabine Oaks that I go and we would go to the hospital on my return.

We were fortunate there was no one in the emergency room at the Medical Center of Southeast Texas in Port Arthur. Winnie was admitted quickly, and tests began to determine her problem. By late afternoon, after a specialist had been called in, she was diagnosed as having a blood clot in her right leg. There was assurance that this could be taken care of. I believe I left the hospital between 6:00 and 7:00 PM. Winnie's spirits had perked up, and we had positive feelings.

Then there was that after-midnight phone call, and you know the rest of the story.

I don't really know how to describe and put into words the many ways Winnie and I traveled together those 51-plus years: all 50 states, Canada, Mexico, and Bermuda. Mostly we traveled together but occasionally with others: Frieda and Joe, Carolyn and Paul, some bus loads, and at least one cold trip to Branson after Thanksgiving with Breanne and a chauffeur named Paul.

Winnie certainly helped me become a whole person. Her love and faith in me, even at times I didn't deserve it, sustained me. Winnie helped me get through a depression and all the things that entails. I don't know the rewards of heaven, but many, many of us are certain she deserves the best.

It is impossible for anyone to understand the vacancy that occurs in one's life when they lose a mate who has been with them for 50-plus years unless one has experienced it. So it was with Beverly and myself. She and Jerry were married longer than Winnie and I. She lost Jerry about six months before Winnie left us. Our relationship began when I invited her to a concert at the Jefferson Theater in Beaumont. We had been friends for a long time, and she had worked at the plant where I was employed.

As our relationship began to form, many apprehensions were experienced. What will people think seeing us together, especially the various friends to Winnie and Jerry? We were amazed as it seemed we were accepted in our own venues and new friendships were formed and a lot of old friendships renewed.

Our friends at our churches, First Baptist Port Neches and Calder Beaumont, embraced us, and we shared many experiences of worship and church activities with each. I must comment that we traveled several times to Branson, Missouri, for the shows and South Texas for the bluebonnets with First Baptist seniors. As an individual couple we enjoyed a Road Scholar event and a Baptist convention in the Carolinas.

I have written about my church experience, but Beverly's was, by and large, a 180-degree difference. She had been a member of First Baptist for most of her life. She had started in the children's department as pianist when she was 16. She had remained in that department through the years to become the leader until she deceased. Sixty-plus years of guidance to every child passing through First Baptist.

Since we lived very close to one another, it was easy to share a lot of time together. I wish I had a mile-a-meter reading on how many miles we walked in the early mornings around Beverly's neighborhood. Beverly and her sons had a garden and fruit trees. I helped and got a good bit of instruction on how to raise tomatoes, okra, peppers, cucumbers, and butter beans. One of her sons raised snap beans and squash to cook and fry. We snapped what he delivered in five-gallon containers.

Another good time was the Friday and/or Saturday night fish fries at Beverly's house with 8 to 20 people in attendance. During spring and fall Beverly's sons, Paul and Tim, supplied the fish. Tim was especially good, fishing at the beach or around the freshwater bayous. Beverly fried, and I did the deep fryer for potatoes, okra, green tomatoes, etc. If fish were not available, we would substitute.

I was reminded of another thing Beverly and I got involved with: grocery store and Dollar Store plastic bags. There is a method of folding and cutting the bags to produce plastic circles or rings. These can then be looped to form a strand of plastic. I believe it was for about a year that Beverly and I cut and looped a huge number of rolls of these bag cuttings. We learned to cut, loop, and watch TV.

There was sense to this madness. The rolls of plastic rope/cord were tendered to a group of woman at First Baptist Church, and they knitted or wove the material into a 3'x5' pad. The pads were bundled together and sent to Africa. My understanding is the pads served as bedding and some of the time were used as birthing pads. We did find things to fill our time.

I was surprised that morning when you and Tammie showed up at my house around 10:30 or 11:00. After we were seated, you explained Beverly had another auto accident and she had serious injuries. As we visited, Lou called and informed you that Beverly had expired. It was shocking to me and difficult to comprehend as I had been with her earlier that morning as she had breakfast and shared she was to play bridge that morning.

One of the outstanding blessings Beverly and I shared was the fact that our children—you Tammie, and Breanne for me; David, Cindy, Paul, and Tim—embraced us and shared time with us.

After Beverly left us, I was once again facing "alone time." Then an unexpected thing happened (I must say a lot of these happenings were unexpected): Carolyn called me. It had been some time since I had been in communication with her. We had attended Paul's, Carolyn's husband, memorial service at the church in Flint, Texas.

Carolyn was seeking advice or, maybe as much as anything, someone to talk too. I was unaware of several things she had faced and found I really knew only a minute part of the problems she was having or had faced.

Paul's stroke in Costa Rica had her dealing with all the problems of getting him back to the States. Carolyn then had been faced with his medical requirements, finally resulting in home care and his passing.

In addition to the above, Carolyn had personal health problems with her heart. This led to multiple catheter ablations (an energy source is inserted and threaded to the heart, where it scars the tissue) and subsequently to the emplacement of a pacemaker. In addition she had a knee operation that led to an infection that brought her to the brink of death.

On top of all this, Paul had not kept her advised, or she had not required a lot of current information concerning their economic status. She assumed they had savings. Paul did not believe in insurance to cover himself but had made arrangement for her being securely covered.

We met, and Carolyn shared some of the difficulties she faced. I began to try to help her deal with a few of the problems. I soon became convinced she needed to get away from the constant worry of the above as well as away from the daily housekeeping and care of her daughter, Kelly, and her husband and two children.

As we were together, both of us began to build a relationship beyond just friends. As you know, our family's friendship with Carolyn goes back to the 1960s.

Carolyn recalls and tells of the incident of you being thrown from the horse and breaking your collarbone. We both have joined in telling of the time when you were four or five years old and all of us—Carolyn, Forrest, Winnie, you and I—were at the restaurant in Beaumont.

If you remember, you needed to go to the bathroom. Winnie and I told you to go, and you took off through the tables. We could see your head as you hurried along out of sight. Very soon, we observed your bobbing head quickly returning to us. It was with deep frustration that you informed all of us, "You know I can't read!"

Winnie and I, along with you, greeted Carolyn and Forrest as they returned from Fort Worth with their adopted son, Forrest III. I seem to remember one time—as you were intrigued by this new arrival and peered through the cradle bars as his diaper was being changed—he gave you a shower. Winnie was a great help in getting Carolyn and Forrest acquainted with being mother and father. Later on, along came Kelly.

I have brought to mind some of the old-time things Carolyn and I shared as we traveled together and I visited in her home and she in mine. I suppose it was inevitable that as we shared and tried to work out some of the problems she faced, we developed a closer relationship.

I believe our relationship fills a need for both of us. As I said to begin with, I dealt with "alone time." I turned my mind to try to understand Carolyn's situation, and my "alone time" began to fill up. As for Carolyn I believe our relationship has given her a positive outlook away from the daily dealing with problems. Although she still deals with extraordinary health problems, she has not allowed these to depress her. We have got her economic situation a little more balanced. This has been a win-win for us.

We would have joined ourselves in marriage, but there are extenuating circumstances that prevent it. We have reconciled our relationship in a manner that causes us to feel blessed in that it reunited us. I cannot perceive what the future holds for us, but she and I are determined to try to make our relationship be one that all of us can embrace.

I have told you that the women of my life are above my pay grade. So it is with Carolyn. She is a very caring and practicing Christian. On top of that, Carolyn is a professional musician. She performs as she was trained—as a pro—whether at a church, retirement facility, or other venue. Carolyn has also chosen to pass along her music talents through those she has taught over the course of 50-plus years.

I have related a little about the women who have contributed to and made my life complete. God has blessed me through them, and God has given them enough patience and love to endure me.

POSTSCRIPT

Son, I have tried to recall, and in most cases retell, a few happenings to me. Some you have recalled. My experiences come from a different time set than you have experienced and are much different from those that have followed you.

We began work earlier in life, so before we were teens, we had learned a little about carpentry, lawnmowing, and gardening. You cannot fully appreciate potatoes if you have not gone down a row of potato vines flicking orangey bugs into a bath of coal-oil.

Starting early in my teen years, I earned my first pay by mowing other families' lawns, applying composition and cedar shingles and an occasion a flat tar roof. These latter things came because Dad was a carpenter, and it also resulted in the fact that I could drive 8 and 16 penny nails about as good as anybody.

Other jobs followed: grocery store (clerk, stocker, and bagger), construction industry (shovel and piling straightener), tire and battery store sales (got fired from that), filling station operator, surveyor's lineman, and drugstore clerk. Everyone worked in the available jobs.

With a work resume like this, I wonder if, as I applied for radar school in the Air Force, someone looked at my resume and thought, "He's got the background to be a flying radar mechanic." Which one tipped the scale?

I write this short note to illustrate how blessed I have been. I received a good high school education and, eventually, a college degree. All of these ventures were due to circumstances I took advantage of or allowed to play out. I was fortunate.

I have to a large extent enjoyed my life and hope to continue letting my memory recall incidences and persons that made it interesting and rewarding.

Papaw

www.ingramcontent.com/pod-product-compliance
Lightning Source LLC
Chambersburg PA
CBHW071005160426
43193CB00012B/1931